P9-DHG-536

MAN'S BEST HERO

Marlborough Public Library
35 West Main Street
Marlborough, MA 01752

ACE COLLINS

MAN'S BEST HERO

TRUE STORIES
OF GREAT AMERICAN DOGS

ABINGDON PRESS
NASHVILLE

Man's Best Hero
True Stories of Great American Dogs

Copyright © 2014 by Ace Collins

All rights reserved.

No part of this work may be reproduced or transmitted in any form or by any means, electronic or mechanical, including photocopying and recording, or by any information storage or retrieval system, except as may be expressly permitted by the 1976 Copyright Act or in writing from the publisher. Requests for permission can be addressed to Permissions, The United Methodist Publishing House, P.O. Box 801, 201 Eighth Avenue South, Nashville, TN 37202-0801, or e-mailed to permissions@umpublishing.org.

Library of Congress Cataloging-in-Publication Data has been requested.

ISBN 978-1-4267-7661-8

14 15 16 17 18 19 20 21 22 23—10 9 8 7 6 5 4 3 2 1

MANUFACTURED IN THE UNITED STATES OF AMERICA

For a great dog trainer who chose to follow
in his father's footsteps,
Bob Weatherwax

CONTENTS

1

OPPORTUNITY

★ ★ ★

THE IMPORTANCE OF SECOND CHANCES

All that is valuable in human society depends upon the opportunity for development accorded the individual.
—*Albert Einstein*

Out of all of the world's creatures, the dog is the one that truly needs to love and serve to be happy and fulfilled. This book focuses on dogs that have earned the title *hero*. Their stories are as varied as their backgrounds. From a four-pound terrier that initiated a mighty movement during World War II, to a massive canine that fought a frigid winter storm to save the man he loved, to a dog that brought hope to those whose spirits were crushed by the terror attacks on September 11, 2001, the animals in these pages have accomplished things far beyond what people believed they could. So in a sense these tales are both inspirational and comforting, but that is not the purpose for placing them in this book. The real reason for telling these amazing stories is to fully present the potential of all dogs, including those in your home right now. All of these canines, be they purebred or mutt, are looking for a calling, yearning to find their potential, and wanting to live out the challenge once issued by the great missionary doctor Albert Schweitzer: "I don't know what your destiny will be, but I do know that the only ones among you who will truly be happy are those who have sought and found how to serve." Thanks to a bit of help from humans, the dogs in this book found a life of service. And that is the challenge for each of us as pet owners. We should not just furnish them a home but also provide our companions with a reason to live.

With that in mind I felt a good place to begin this book was not by focusing on a dog but on a person who loves both dogs and humans. Through faith, determination, vision, and persistence, she has found a way to give the animals no one wanted and the people deemed unforgiveable a second chance at life. And that is a theme found throughout this book—second chances.

Beautiful, tall, and elegant, on first glance Renie Rule defines sophistication and grace. She could be the model for the modern businesswoman. But so much more than her career defines her. Rule possesses charismatic warmth that draws you right into her soul and a spirit that inspires those around her to dig deeper and climb higher. Robert F. Kennedy once said, "There are those who look at things and ask why, I dream of things that never were and ask why not." Rule is one of those rare people who constantly finds answers to problems others usually fail to see.

The Fort Worth native and Little Rock resident is the executive director of the University of Arkansas for Medical Sciences. And though her activities in helping to guide one of the nation's top teaching hospitals are remarkable, it is her job of transforming lives through volunteer work that has seen her create a new breed of heroes. These all but unnoticed champions were once unwanted canines that were on their way to doggy death row but now serve as assistance animals, therapy dogs, and pets. Her revolutionary work has touched thousands, and it was remarkably born out of one sad man's final request.

Rule's upbringing as a missionary's kid gave her a slightly different point of view than most folks. After watching her parents work in some of the poorest areas on the globe and live out their passion for service each day of their lives, Rule doesn't look for what she can take but rather searches for what she can give. Even as a child in Brazil she was saving starving dogs while her parents were feeding hungry people. Perhaps it was those actions that gave her the conviction that every animal and person, no matter what they have done in the past, has the potential to be something remarkable now and in the future.

In the summer of 1994, Rule was forty-four when she read a newspaper story about Hoyt Franklin Clines. Clines was on death row awaiting execution for robbery and murder. In his final interview he told a reporter he had hoped his last meal would be a hamburger, French fries, and banana bread. The first two were easy requests for the prison to fill, but the prisoner was deeply disappointed when he was informed the unit's kitchen could not make banana bread.

Most people would have read the story and felt little compassion for a man society had deemed unfit to live, but not Renie Rule. She went to the store, bought the necessary ingredients, raced back to her kitchen, mixed and baked the bread, and then drove more than an hour to deliver it to the prison gate. At that moment she had no way of knowing this simple act would lead to starting a program that would radically change the lives of dogs and humans on both sides of prison walls. All she was doing was trying to show compassion for one single soul.

On August 2, the night before he was to be executed, Clines was allowed to make a phone call. For almost an hour the lonely man spoke with Rule. As the conversation was ending she asked him if there was anything else she could do during his last day on earth. The man quickly replied, "Will you build a chapel down here?"

There would be no appeal; Clines met his maker in the death chamber the next night, but his wishes did not die with him. Over the next few years Rule raised the funds and cut the red tape to build a simple chapel in the state's Varner Unit prison. When the small, cinderblock building was completed, she placed a sign over the door that says, "Bless all who enter." To the prisoners Rule's act of kindness seemed almost unbelievable, but to the missionary's daughter it was nothing more than living out the biblical passage that had defined her parents' life and work—Matthew 25:35-40.

"For I was hungry and you gave me something to eat, I was thirsty and you gave me something to drink, I was a stranger and you invited me in, I needed clothes and you clothed me, I was sick and you looked after me, I was in prison and you came to visit me."

"Then the righteous will answer him, 'Lord, when did we see you hungry and feed you, or thirsty and give you something to drink? When did we see you a stranger and invite you in, or needing clothes and clothe you? When did we see you sick or in prison and go to visit you?'

"The King will reply, 'Truly I tell you, whatever you did for one of the least of these brothers and sisters of mine, you did for me.'"

Rule could have walked away after constructing the chapel, but she didn't. Instead she began to look deeply into the prison system. As she went behind the walls and observed what life was like in this sterile, loveless, and often brutal environment, she saw things others on the inside and outside missed—potential and hope. And she had seen those same qualities in another very sad place she had visited—the local animal shelter. Rule wondered what would happen if she could find a way to take people no one believed in and connect them to dogs no one wanted. After putting the concept into a detailed plan, she set a goal of making it happen.

Rule took the idea to Governor Mike Beebe, and the dog owner immediately approved it. She then went to Arkansas Department of Corrections Director Ray Hobbs with her plan, and he embraced it. Then it was time to really get the ball rolling. After a team studied the Missouri Department of Correction's Puppies for Parole program and Rule raised the money through private donations to fund the program, Paws in Prison was born. It had taken years of work and planning, but Rule had found a way to give unwanted dogs a second chance at life and provide unwanted people an opportunity to find purpose.

As per Rule's original vision, Paws in Prison partners with shelters and rescue groups to bring unwanted dogs into prison to live with the inmates. The inmates and dogs work with professional dog trainers once a week and then practice the skills they have learned between sessions. The training goes well beyond house breaking, socialization, and basic obedience work. Dogs are also taught to read commands and respond to flash cards, help with taking off jackets and untying shoes, turn light switches on and off, and retrieve a wide variety of household items. Their training is so extensive some of the dogs graduate knowing more than a hundred different commands.

The men and women who train these dogs also have to meet

rigid standards. They must live up to a certain code of conduct and work well with others. They must prove their kindness and respect for the prison staff before they are given an animal. Some of those who have stepped into the role of dog trainers have long rap sheets that include crimes such as murder and kidnapping. Many were once considered men and women who could not be reformed or rehabilitated. That all changed when the dogs came to visit. The convicts in this program live to love, and the dogs they train take that love to the world in a wide variety of remarkable ways.

One canine graduate of the program is now assisting a boy who has cerebral palsy and uses a wheelchair. Another attends college with her wheelchair-bound adopted mom. Several dogs are used in reading programs in elementary schools and others have become the hands of men and women badly injured in war. They are pets and therapy dogs. They serve in homes and hospitals. They are teachers and mentors. And this transformation from unwanted and discarded dog to valued family member of society began under the tutelage of people most had deemed worthless.

The program Rule was inspired to create now operates at the Maximum Security Unit at Tucker, the Ouachita River Correctional Unit in Malvern, the North Central Unit at Calico Rock, Randall Williams Correctional Facility in Pine Bluff, and the Hawkins Center for Women in Wrightsville and the Tucker Unit. This program has saved hundreds of dogs from euthanasia while touching thousands of human lives. Yet what these unwanted canines have done outside the walls pales in comparison to what they have accomplished inside the prison units.

Their impact behind the bars goes beyond heroism and into the area reserved for miracles.

She was an attractive, dark-haired woman with little hope and less direction and had already served a fifteen-year stretch when she saw the first dog brought into her prison unit. The diminutive, slightly built young woman, who had literally lived half her life behind walls, was suddenly flooded with long-forgotten memories of one of the few happy moments from her troubled youth. In a life filled with abuse and neglect, there had been a single steady friend she could trust—a stray dog that had somehow found and befriended her. As she studied the wagging tail and happy face of the new prison arrival, she wondered if the spirit of the dog that had once loved her unconditionally could be found in this visitor too.

The female prisoner met with Rule and the professional trainer and asked to be placed in the Paws in Prison program. When accepted, she quickly proved to be more than just a solid trainer; she was gifted. While behind bars she prepared animals as pets and assistance dogs and grew so good at her craft she was certified as a professional canine trainer. When this once-directionless woman left prison, she immediately found work with one of the nation's top pet supply companies as a master trainer. The dogs who lived in prison with her did not just give her a reason to live, they paved a new life filled with purpose and joy.

Another miracle happened when a big, broad-shouldered solemn man with a deep sadness in his eyes saw the dogs first walked into his unit. This middle-aged ex-Marine had once served his country with honor and had been recognized as one of his nation's finest soldiers. Yet after he returned from several tours in the Middle East, he had problems dealing with everyday life. An anger and rage that he could not control began to boil in his gut. He fought demons he could not see or understand, and one night he didn't walk away from a confrontation and killed a man.

Locked away in prison with little hope of ever tasting freedom again, the former Marine was eaten up with guilt. Deeply troubled by the shame he had brought to his family and the branch of the service he had been so proud to call his own, he could barely look at himself in the mirror. Worst of all, there was nothing he could begin to do to once again serve others in a positive way.

Paws in Prison gave the brooding man something to focus on. When he asked if he could become a part of the program, he was told he could earn his way there through his attitude and behavior. He did. And now the man who will never again taste freedom trains dogs for roles as assistants to other Marines who came back from war severely handicapped. His trained canines are opening doors and providing new opportunities for men and women who had thought their lives were over.

Another of the program's remarkable trainers was in his fifties when he saw his first Paws in Prison dog. Short, graying, slightly stooped, the man had spent almost his entire adult life behind bars. Because of three different violent crimes, he knew he would not get out from behind the walls until he died. With this depressing reality holding him in a vice-like grip, he had given up. Over the past decade he had even lost his ability to walk and now had to use a wheelchair. He was totally dependent upon the staff and other prisoners for even his most basic needs.

When those around him began to train dogs, he asked the warden if he could become a part of the program. The answer was an immediate no. A man in a wheelchair could not do what was necessary to train a dog to be a service animal or even a pet.

A month later this now-determined man stood for the first time in a decade and took his first steps in a walker. When he found out that was not enough, he worked harder. In just eight weeks he was walking. A month later he was able to run and he earned his way into the program.

This lifer has trained half a dozen dogs that have become incredible family pets. He has worked with small animals and big ones, those that were high energy and those that moved slowly, shy dogs and outgoing canines, and those that were beautiful and others that weren't. And all of them had one thing in common with him. They too had been discarded and given up on by society.

In these three cases and scores of others, Renie Rule's vision has given both dogs and convicts a reason to live. Paws in Prison has also become one of the most remarkable rehabilitation programs in the nation. Those who once defied authority suddenly found peace, security, and value through the love of shelter dogs. By teaming unwanted people with unwanted canines, Rule gave both a reason to live and love.

Several years ago, my wife and I were moved to adopt a beautiful male collie. As I looked at this rescue dog I found it amazing that most felt he should be put down. What was his crime? He was born completely blind.

Sammy has become one of the most remarkable animals I have ever met. He is able to navigate our home as well as any sighted dog. He can chase squirrels and still miss every tree in our yard. He is gentle, compassionate, and loving. And he is always smiling. I have never seen an animal or human enjoy life as much as does Sammy. This blind dog that most felt should be put down is my hero because he teaches me and so many others that there is no reason to limit ourselves because of others' perceptions. In his time with us he has inspired countless folks not just to see the potential of special-needs dogs but also to be better people.

Renie Rule did more than start a program; she created heroes out of dogs no one wanted. We have that potential too. We can help dogs become more than just companions; like the dogs that go behind bars and like Sammy at our house, they can be our teachers, spiritual guides, and even our heroes.

Several years ago I was asked to identify the best role model I had ever met. I smiled and quickly answered, "Lassie." Why? Because Lassie lives a life filled with love, courage, forgiveness, compassion, and acceptance. And every dog has that same potential. If you don't believe me, then go meet the unwanted canines that have been trained by those who are a part of Paws in Prison! Dogs are more than pets; they are modest and unassuming heroes in the making that are just waiting for the opportunity to awe in ways we cannot begin to imagine.

2

TENACITY

★ ★ ★

HE NEVER SURRENDERED

Let me tell you the secret that has led me to my goal.
My strength lies solely in my tenacity.
—Louis Pasteur

It had been just over a year since John F. Kennedy had been gunned down in Dallas, Texas, and the country was still immersed in a cloud of confusion. The great social upheaval that was sweeping America was being covered by television. Millions were bombarded daily by events that seemed to shake traditional thinking to the core. A young, suddenly politically active generation was protesting against the war in Vietnam. African Americans, inspired by Martin Luther King, Jr., were marching in the streets demanding equal rights. The Beatles and other British acts controlled the music industry pushing Elvis, Sinatra, and other U.S. artists to the back burner. TV and movies were beginning to take on an edge that left many people uncomfortable. America's sense of greatness and opportunity that had defined the 1950s had given way to a period of 1960s pessimism. This dark cloud of insecurity and apprehension had invaded every corner of the country including Tacoma, Washington. It seemed what America needed was a born-and-bred hero but what the country had was a crop of anti-heroes. In many ways this was a sad and depressing time.

With Christmas just days away, Marvin Scott, a gray-haired man in his sixties, was trying to ignore the national malaise and praying his furniture business would pick up. Scott's dark-rimmed glasses, black, conservative suit, white shirt, and muted tie made the Tacoma store owner appear almost as gloomy as the national mood. Yet far from being a somber, withdrawn person, Scott was actually outgoing and charming. He had a zest for life that few men nearing retirement age possessed. Though usually hidden by his dark coats, he possessed broad, rugged shoulders and a flat stomach that also proved his vibrant and inexhaustible energy. Because of having to move the heavy furniture he sold, he was also a strong man who retained his optimism when it seemed the whole country had chosen to embrace a cynical spirit. Though he didn't know it, he would need each of those traits and a remarkable dog to just survive until the holidays.

Scott lived in one of the most beautiful places in the country. Spanaway, Washington, sprang to life in the 1890s as a tourist resort. Back then people from all over the world took the train to the small community to visit Mt. Rainer. As the visitors got off at the train station, the picturesque, snow-covered mountain loomed in the background leaving them in awe. Most snapped photos and bought postcards and took the story of the area back to places like Kansas City, Chicago, Dallas, and New York. A few decided the area was so breathtaking they wanted to see it each morning when they awoke. Hence, over time, the small town was transformed into a quaint community filled with people who loved outdoor life.

Over the decades Marvin Scott watched the town grow and prosper while also keeping an eye on the unchanging Mt. Rainer. He often spent hours on the dock just three hundred yards before his lakefront home relishing the incredible vistas nature presented to him. What he saw while enjoying Lake Spanaway never grew old. And usually when he was on the dock or walking around the lake, Scott was accompanied by a mutt named Patches.

Patches was anything but a purebred dog. The white-and-brown fifty-pound mass of fur defined the term "medium-sized mongrel." Scott freely acknowledged his canine was a mix of collie and malamute with likely a few other things tossed in, but the man believed that gave the dog character. In an age where everyone wanted a certain breed and was paying big bucks for that privilege, the furniture store owner took special pride in having an animal no one would pay money to own. In Scott's way of thinking, Patches defined America and its individual spirit.

From the collie side of his family, Patches had developed a real instinct for herding. The problem was Scott didn't own any sheep, goats, or cows. So the dog constantly tried to unsuccessfully corral the ducks and geese that lived around the lake. He also leaned into Scott when they walked together.

From the malamute side, Patches received a stubborn nature that caused Scott even more grief than having the dog try to herd him on their walks. Malamutes simply have a mind of their own. Much like a cat, they decide which of their master's orders were important and which could be ignored. Added to this independent streak was brute strength. Malamutes had been bred for generations for to pull heavy freight across Alaska's deep snow, so the dog was as strong as he was stubborn.

Tough but not large, Patches was also tenacious. Once he set his mind to something he stuck with it. That meant if he decided to drag a large piece of driftwood up the steep, rock-covered bank to Scott's home he would not rest until the task was completed. It mattered not to the dog that his human companion returned the wood to the lake almost as soon as it had appeared at the back-door. Added to these malamute traits was the collie's ability to problem solve. That meant the dog could figure out how to open latches thus getting into places he wasn't supposed to be.

Winter was Patches's least favorite season. He didn't mind the cold weather; in fact, with his dual coats he thrived in it. What he hated were the short days. Having so little daylight meant that he and Scott couldn't spend as much time down by the lake, and the dog sorely missed those bonding moments with his master.

On this December night it was just past ten and the temperature had already fallen to single digits when Patches noted the sound of Scott's approaching car. Shaking the sleep from his head, the dog got up and ambled to the front door. After patting Patches's head and then visiting with his wife, Scott moved to the kitchen window to glance down at the lake. He could make out the form of a patrol boat, almost hidden in the darkness, tied up at their dock. The almost gale-force winds appeared to be knocking it against the side of the pier. He wondered out loud if he needed to go down to the lake and do a better job securing the craft. His wife quickly assured him that it was a night not fit for man or beast and he should stay inside and let the local officers worry about their boat. She added that if it was no concern to them it should not be a concern to him either. As the woman would soon discover, those words of wisdom went in one ear and out the other.

Scott ate a late supper, glanced through the mail, and turned on the TV. Sitting in his chair he tried to relax but every time he heard the wind his thoughts took him back to the lake. Maybe the government folks weren't worried about their boat but that didn't mean he shouldn't be concerned about the dock and pier. The wind, icing on the lake, and cold weather spelled a combination for disaster and, if he could prevent any damage from happening, he felt he should do it. The wind chill was well below zero; he fought the urge to act on his impulse for almost half an hour. Finally, at eleven, he looked over to his wife and announced he was at least going to go down to the lake and check on things. Putting on a heavy coat over his suit, grabbing his gloves and a hat, he walked out the back door into the unforgiving cold. By his side, ducking his head down low toward the ground to try and avoid the wind, was an eager and enthusiastic Patches. In the dog's mind it was never too cold for a walk.

The rocks that covered the dramatically sloping ground leading to the lake helped prevent erosion, but tonight those tiny boulders made walking all but impossible. Scott's dress shoes slipped with each of his steps. Several times he barely caught himself before falling. He was a third of the way to the water when he wondered if maybe his wife had been right. Perhaps what happened to the boat and pier didn't matter. Yet as he turned back to look at the house the climb up appeared even less inviting than the walk down.

Though much more nimble than the man, Patches was sliding too. More than once the icy rocks' uneven size and shape, combined with the strong, cold breeze sent the dog sprawling. Yet, unlike the man, he never looked back. His eyes were on the prize—a chance to walk around the lake with his master.

It took more than ten minutes for the two to make their way to the dock but only a few seconds for Scott to realize he had been right. The wind was pushing the boat against the pier. He needed to find a way to shove it back out into the lake a bit and wedge an object between the vessel and wood to protect them both. As he got closer something else caught his eye. The wind had blown lake water onto the side of the boat and dock and it was now frozen. If that layer grew thick enough it could do great damage to both.

Standing uneasily on the dock, leaning into the wind to keep his balance, his glasses now freezing over with spray, Scott fully appreciated just how cold it was. It was as if the wind was blowing right through the layers of clothing and to his skin. As he took a deep breath of the moist air even his lungs began to ache. Whatever he needed to do, he had to do it quickly and get back to the house. If he didn't he might be a candidate for frostbite.

Looking around he noted a small limb that had been pushed onto shore. Carefully making his way to it, he picked it up. It was well over four feet long, so it had the length he needed. It was also thick enough to do the job. Sliding across the frozen ground and back onto the pier, he skated toward the boat's stern. Trying to lock his feet on the wooden planking, he aimed the timber at the boat and gave a powerful shove. Because the lake surface's was now an almost invisible sheet of ice, the boat held solid. That should have been a sign for the man to simply give up and head home, but like his dog, the businessman also had a deep stubborn streak. He simply could not stop in the middle of a job; he had to finish it.

Just behind Scott, his coat bristling in an effort to fight off the wind and cold, Patches observed the man's futile efforts. Pawing at the icy deck, the dog moved closer as if trying to understand the purpose in this exercise. Just as he sidled up beside the man's leg, Scott again pushed against the boat. Once more the vessel was held solidly in place by the frozen water, but this time the man was not so fortunate. His leather soles lost their grip on the wooden planks, and he began sliding backwards. Tossing the timber to one side, Scott attempted to straighten up. Stretching his arms to gain balance, his body twisted. From the corner of his eye he spied the end of the pier and the floating dock that rested alongside it. If he didn't find a way to stop he realized he would be falling the six feet down to the dock.

Time slowed down to a crawl. Looking around he tried to find something to grab to stop his awkward slide. Except for Patches, whose face was framed in a combination of amusement and fascination, he saw nothing. Flapping his arms in the air as if trying to fly, Scott made one final turn before sliding off the frozen pier. The man was only airborne for a split second before crashing feet first to wooden, floating dock. As he landed the pain was immediate and searing. It felt as if his legs had been caught in a vise and were being slowly crushed. What he didn't know at that moment was that he had torn all the tendons, ligaments, and muscles from his knees to his ankles. Screaming in agony, Scott attempted to roll over. This move pushed him off the dock and into the lake, where he crashed through a thin layer of ice.

The shock of the frigid water stunned Scott so badly it took his breath away. His mind was now working in slow motion and his thoughts were jumbled. Glancing to his left his eyes focused on the deck. It was getting further away. That meant the wind and current were pushing out into the middle of the lake. If he did not get back to shore in a matter of minutes, he would either die of exposure or drown. Instinct demanded he kick his legs and swim back to shore. His brain immediately sent that message to his legs but as they attempted to follow the command unfathomable pain shot up his spine and hips all but causing him to lapse into unconsciousness. Fighting to hold on to his wits, Scott tried to tread water, but the water had now soaked through all the layers of his clothing, and the weight of those garments was dragging him down into the twenty-foot-deep channel.

After taking one last gasp of frigid air, Scott sank under the waves and into the darkness below the thin ice. The pain from his injuries numbed his will to fight, and the cold demanded he accept what fate held for him. Slowly his mind began to process that he was going to die in the lake he loved so dearly. How long would it take them to find his body? Who would come out into the frigid weather and make the search? Would anyone ever really know what had happened?

A few feet away, his dark-brown eyes glued to the spot in the water where Scott had gone under, a perplexed Patches watched. Leaping down from the pier to the dock, the dog slipped and fell on his belly. It took several moments for him to dig his claws through the ice on the wood and regain his footing. Rushing over to the place where Scott had rolled off the planking, the dog studied the water, took a deep breath, and plunged in. Paddling over to the spot where the man had disappeared, the dog took another deep gasp and dove under the waves.

Scott was slipping into an almost comalike trance when he felt something grab his hair. A second later he felt his whole body being yanked toward the surface. When he emerged from what he had assumed would be his watery grave, he took a deep breath and tried to refocus. Reaching up, he felt Patches's wide head.

The dog's jaw had a firm grasp on the man's graying but thankfully thick head of hair. For the moment he was safe, but as the wind was pushing them farther from the shore, they were still facing a huge challenge.

In order to breathe, Scott needed to roll over onto his back. Patches seemed to sense that and let go of the man's hair, but as soon as Scott had deeply inhaled, filling his lungs with the frosty air, the dog once more took ahold of the man's hair and began to paddle back toward the shore. Not only was Patches battling the wind but he was also breaking the ice with his feet and chest as he moved forward. Yet the tenacity that often got him into trouble now pushed him stubbornly forward. He would die before he gave up. The distance the dog had to cover was only twenty feet, but because of the conditions and the man's weight, it took almost five minutes to it make it back to the place where Scott had slipped into the lake.

Patches swam beside the dock, allowing Scott's body to bump up against the floating wooden structure. Though dazed and confused, the man finally understood what the dog wanted. Gripping the dock's edge with his hands, Scott slowly yanked himself out of the lake. Rolling over, he quickly realized the dog had not followed.

Patches was so exhausted he could no longer move. He had used every bit of energy just to save the man. Now he was floundering in the water. Grabbing the dog by the scruff of the neck, Scott somehow found the strength to pull him to safety, but as he did, the man lost his balance and fell back into the icy abyss.

Panting on the deck, Patches watched his master plunge back into the water. Totally exhausted, the dog surely realized that he had done all he could do. Yet for reasons no human has ever understood, the dog, fully aware it likely meant he was going to die, pulled himself off the dock and leaped back into the icy lake.

Scott had now blacked out. Diving under the surface, Patches again found the man's hair. Latching onto it with his solid jaw, the canine rotated and headed back toward the surface. Breaking out of the water, he regained his bearings and began to paddle toward shore. Again Patches stopped at the dock until he saw Scott reach up and grab onto the side. The dog then swam to shore, pulled himself of the water, ran out onto the pier, leaped down to the dock, and slid over to the man. The now nearly frozen furniture owner was shocked when Patches leaned forward, grabbed the back of the man's coat collar, dug his claws into the ice, and yanked. It took several minutes for Patches to get Scott out of the water. Not satisfied to simply pull up on the deck, this time the dog kept tugging until he had the man in the middle of the floating wooden structure.

Exhausted and unable to walk, Scott rolled over onto his back and screamed for help. On a normal night at least a dozen people would have heard him and come down to investigate. But because of the cold all the windows were latched tight. After a few minutes with no response, the man took a deep breath and gave up. Among all the thoughts racing through his mind was that no one would ever realize what Patches had done that night.

The man might have given in, but the dog hadn't. After a short rest, Patches got up and called on his malamute breeding and his collie problem solving. Grabbing Scott's collar, the dog yanked him a foot forward. Jarred awake by the canine's efforts, the man rolled over and used his elbows to move a foot on his own. That small movement took almost all the man's energy. As he rested the dog yanked Scott off the dock and onto the shore. The dog was simply not going to give up until the man was safely home.

Beyond the pain from his horrific injuries, the numbing cold was starting to play with the man's mind. It was demanding he give up. Again and again a voice inside his brain yelled at him to just let things be. After all, he was out of the water, his body would be easy to find and no one would have to risk their lives looking for him. But each moment he was about to close his eyes and check out, Patches sank his teeth into the heavy coat collar and dragged him a few more feet.

There was no path from the lake to his house. The rocks made going straight up the hill difficult even in the best of times. Tonight the large stones would have been almost impossible to manage for both a healthy man and rested beast. But somehow Patches's stubborn spirit drove him on. Foot by foot he dragged the man higher up the steep hill. When he grew too weary to move, he laid down beside Scott to warm him. Once he'd rested a bit, he got up, faced the wind, and went back to work. Inspired by his efforts, Scott found new strength and grabbed onto the rocks to help. Together the duo slowly moved up the hill.

Back in the house, Mrs. Scott walked over to the kitchen window and glanced down toward the dock. The patrol boat was still there but there was no sign of her husband. A tinge of concern raced through her body, but she figured he had likely gone next door to see if the friendly neighbors could help him secure the craft. Besides, if anything had happened, Patches would have come home. The fact the mutt was not scratching at the door must mean that everything was all right, she thought.

Scott looked up and saw his wife at the window. He cried out to her, but the wind carried his voice away. She never heard him. And because he was dressed in dark clothes he was sure she couldn't have seen him either. But he was now too close to give up.

Knowing that home was now within reach provided Scott and Patches with a second wind. As the man grabbed onto the rocks with more vigor, the dog now pulled more and rested less. Patches was completely exhausted when he finally made it to the grass in the family's backyard. After grabbing the man's coat collar a final time and managing to bring Scott another six inches closer to home, the weary canine collapsed.

The cold had numbed the pain to the point where Scott was once again drifting into unconsciousness. But he had to at least live long enough to tell the story of Patches's courage and fortitude. Using the last bit of reasoning power he could muster, he grabbed a rock and heaved it toward the back of the house. The pebble hit the kitchen window just as his wife walked by. This time, when she looked outside, she spotted Scott in the yard. A few moments later she was by his side. After dragging him out of the cold, she called an ambulance. Worried about her husband, unable to comprehend his injuries, she ignored the dog that had literally saved the man's life three times in the past hour. She had no idea the only reason Scott was alive was because the wet, smelly canine now resting in the living room had brought him home.

At Tacoma General Hospital, Marvin Scott's injuries were assessed. His legs were in horrible shape. The doctors didn't even know if he would ever be able to walk again. But for the moment that was the least of the problems. Scott was suffering from hypothermia and frostbite. Because of the water he had ingested during his period in the lake, his lungs were damaged as well. Within hours the doctors' worst fears were realized as he developed pneumonia.

With infections raging through his body and medications masking his excruciating pain, Scott was out of his head for days. Hovering on the edge between life and death he would spend Christmas and New Year's in the hospital. Meanwhile, back at home, Patches, unaware of what had happened to his master, anxiously waited for him to come home. And finally, after several major surgeries and twenty-seven days in the hospital, Scott did come home. It was only then that family and friends were made fully aware of Patches's life-saving efforts.

The dog stayed by the man's side as he recovered, but it would be six months before Scott was able to use two canes and walk back to the dock. Beside him each step of the way was the dog that wouldn't let him die.

In the annals of canine history there have been thousands of dogs that have saved people's lives. Some of the famous names lionized in dog lore include Balto, Tang, Duke, Ringo, and Bear. Still, for many dog lovers, there is one dog that, due to his incredible determination, devotion, and fortitude, stands head and shoulders above the rest. At a time when America's fiber was being rocked by insecurity and changed, when faith and hope were rare, in one hour, with no hesitation or concern for his own welfare, Patches proved his heroic nature three times. If there was a canine Medal of Honor, this dog's image should be on it and if there was a dog that defined the essence of the American spirit and will to survive even the toughest times, it was this collie/malamute mutt. When the country needed a hero, Patches answered the call.

3

DETERMINATION

★ ★ ★

EXCEEDING EVERY EXPECTATION

*The difference between the impossible and the possible
lies in a man's determination.*
—Tommy Lasorda

It would be World War II before the United States military began to train dogs for active duty. During that era dogs drafted into service were almost always German shepherds. Reflecting the qualities of canine movie heroes Strongheart and Rin Tin Tin, the large, powerful, athletic, singular-minded, and determined breed was the poster boy of dog heroism. The connection with the military was so strong that in 1942 when Uncle Sam said, "I want you," he was usually pointing to a German shepherd.

Yet, in World War I, long before the army or marines had even considered using dogs in combat, a fifteen-pound, stubby-tailed, black, brindle, and seal-colored Boston terrier charmed his way into the hearts of new recruits. He was nothing like the dogs used in later wars, but this fiery little mutt proved that it was not the size of the dog in the fight, but the size of the fight in the dog that mattered in life and in the army. He was an unlikely hero, but in military annals this diminutive mutt has no rivals.

Nothing is known of Stubby's first months of life, but there is little doubt that he was lost or abandoned when still a very small pup. Pugnacious, cute, but in a very ugly sort of way, in his build and appearance he was very likely a purebred Boston terrier. As the breed was very popular on the east coast in the first few decades of the 1900s, it was not uncommon for those dogs that could not be sold to be dumped. And as the country was literally overrun with unwanted dogs, few ever found homes. But even though he was adrift and alone, this feisty creature found a way to beat the odds and survive. In fact, his will to live and ability to adapt would be the key to hundreds of Americans coming home after World War I.

When folks first started noticing the terrier he was making daily rounds digging through trash in New Haven, Connecticut. He was a loner who usually stuck to the alleys, watched cars, carriages, and people from a distance, and stayed away from other dogs. Those who began to observe the canine grew to admire his attitude. He was smart enough to avoid dogcatchers and quick enough to outrun housewives armed with brooms. His stride was strong and he carried his head high. Even though he was completely unwanted and had no human friends, the little creature most called a bulldog still acted as though he was king of the walk.

Stubby might have stayed on the streets if he hadn't made a side trip to Yale University. It was late fall and he was looking for food under the stands of the football field when a group of army recruits assembled in the stadium to begin their marching exercises. Fascinated by what he observed, the dog walked out to the side of the gridiron, took a seat, and followed the action. He remained completely mesmerized for the next two hours.

Though no one knew why, watching the men training at Yale for the war in Europe became a part of Stubby's daily routine. Sensing they had a fan, some of the men began to bring kitchen scraps to the little mutt. Within a week, due to his sawed-off tail, he had been given the name "Stubby." The aloof dog even began to bond with several of the men. As he grew to trust them, the recruits played with the dog and even let him stay in their tents. Once Stubby was fully entrenched in the camp, Corporal Robert Conroy took over the care of the newest army recruit. Beyond feeding Stubby, Conroy's primary job was making sure the commanding officers never caught sight of the little guy.

As it neared the time for 102nd to ship out, Stubby was no longer content to just watch the troopers drill. One day, to the horror of Conroy and his mates, the terrier joined them on the parade grounds. Marking perfectly square turns and holding his head high, the dog brought up the rear of the formation. When the drill sergeant called for the unit to halt and turn to face the observing officer, the dog did as well, holding his pose as if waiting for the command "at ease." When that order finally came, the little dog sat down. As Conroy and his friends whispered, urging Stubby to run away, one of the commanding officers made his way toward the dog.

"What have we here?" he demanded.

"Just a stray dog," Conroy explained. Then he quickly admitted, "He's hanging around because we've been feeding him scraps."

"That is against regulations," the officer pointed out.

"Yes, sir," the corporal acknowledged.

The officer leaned toward the terrier, shook his head, and yelled, "Someone get this dog out of here."

The words had no more than left the man's lips when Stubby sat up on his haunches and raised his right paw to his brow as if he were saluting. A few giggles were heard as the officer shook his head and frowned. But, when the dog continued to hold the salute, even the career military man grinned. Finally, not really knowing what else to do, he shrugged and barked, "At ease." Stubby immediately dropped back to a standing position.

"Conroy," the officer said, "come over here." After the corporal joined him, the officer whispered, "You can keep the dog until we ship out. But don't abandon it when you leave. Find this guy a good home."

For the next two weeks Stubby was the unofficial mascot of the 102nd. He not only slept in a cot but ate in the mess hall. He also continued to salute all the company's officers. But when it came time for the group to board a troop train south, heading for the ship that would take them overseas, Conroy had grown so fond of the dog he disobeyed orders. Rather than seek out a local family to adopt the dog, he hid Stubby in his gear. The dog remained hidden through the train trip to the coast. Once at the dock the corporal snuck the dog past the military police and onto the ship. At the time his motivation was only based on his love for the animal, he had no idea that his illegal and very unmilitary actions would result in saving the lives of countless men during some of the fiercest battles of the war.

The ship was miles out to sea before Conroy brought Stubby out on deck. As the men watched and laughed, the small dog went through a range of tricks including saluting one of the naval officers. The ship's machinist mate was so impressed with the terrier he not only allowed him to stay in his quarters but also made the pooch a set of dog tags. When the ship finally arrived in Europe and the men departed for the battlefront, Stubby, who according to his tags had been promoted to sergeant, marched with them as the official mascot of the Yankee Division of the 102nd.

On February 5, 1918, Stubby and his company found themselves facing German fire for the first time at Chemin des Dames. The taste of real war was nothing like the glamorous adventures the men had been promised by army recruiters. The conditions were horrible. They lived, ate, slept, and fought in trenches. They were so close to the enemy they could hear them talking. Constant rain made the trenches foul mud pits. The front line went back and forth on a daily basis and just holding a piece of ground for twenty-four hours was considered a success.

Conroy and the others, who had been told this experience would be a short European vacation and when the Americans arrived the Germans would race back to Berlin, found that war really was hell. They watched men die ghastly deaths. They observed soldiers snap under the pressure and race out of the trenches into machine gunfire. But there was no turning back; no matter how many died or were wounded, each day both sides kept firing their weapons and prolonging a war that now seemed endless.

In the midst of this hell on earth, Stubby offered the men in the trenches unbridled love. Their mascot transformed himself into a morale officer. As such, Stubby was often more important than letters from home. The dog that barked encouragement during the battles sat in the soldiers' laps during breaks. He shared their meals and listened to their fears. He never complained. The terrier's gentle licks also soothed mental wounds that often ran deeper than physical injuries.

In April, the 102nd was given the task of taking the French town of Schieprey. As always, Stubby was at Conroy's side. Early in the day, the Americans' push rooted the Germans out of their position. As the enemy retreated they lobbed hand grenades back toward the rushing allied soldiers. A piece of shrapnel caught Stubby in the right foreleg and chest, knocking the terrier to the ground. Rolling over, the dog regained his footing and limped forward on three legs beside the advancing 102nd. Barking as he moved, he continued to stubbornly push forward until the battle ended. It was then Conroy got Stubby to the medics. They patched the dog up the best they could and shipped him back to a field hospital. There the pooch received the same care and attention as his human companions.

During his six weeks spent convalescing, Stubby entertained the men in the field hospital. He performed the series of tricks Conroy had taught him, always saluted visiting officers and became a favorite with the nurses. He posed for pictures, was the spotlighted subject of several of the letters to home and even crawled up and slept beside men who were deathly ill. In a few cases, Stubby's small head was the last thing these men touched before they died. Doctors called him a hero for lifting spirits, but patients knew him more as an angel. His wet nose and gentle touch reminded them of their own dogs and home. In a sense, his daily rounds through the wards gave desperate men something to look forward to and live for.

Newspapers picked up on the exploits of the 102nd's mascot and the little guy's story found its ways across France and into publications in England and the United States. Thanks to the press coverage, by the time Stubby was declared well enough to return to his unit he had become a minor celebrity. But the dog's war role was about to dramatically change. Just like men such as Alvin York, Stubby was about to see needs and grow to fill them.

During the summer, while staying in the trenches with the men, Stubby and the Americans were exposed to a killer that silently snuck behind the lines to strangle its victims. Sulfur mustards, more commonly known as mustard gas, were delivered in a wide variety of methods. Often men were completely unaware they had been exposed to the substance. If enough of the gas was ingested, a victim would die, but, even in small doses, the weapon had long-term effects on the body and mind. Once absorbed, the gas caused a wide variety of issues from lesions on the lungs to open body wounds. A nurse who worked in a field hospital described the way the victims suffered, "They cannot be bandaged or touched. We cover them with a tent of propped-up sheets. Gas burns must be agonizing because usually the other cases do not complain, even with the worst wounds, but gas cases are invariably beyond endurance and they cannot help crying out." Those who survived the attacks often begged to die and those who died spent their last days in unbearable agony.

The gas that rolled into the trench where Stubby and the 102nd were fighting was a silent invader. The dog was the first to show the signs, as he began coughing and rolling in the dirt. Soon the men began itching and complaining their skin was on fire. Medics could do nothing and the victims were hurriedly shipped back to a hospital. Some of those exposed that day would die and many more would be unable to return to active duty. Even the men who managed to shake the effects would later have a myriad of health issues often including cancer.

Stubby was one of the lucky ones. Perhaps because he was low to the ground, he experienced only mild reactions to the gas. Within a couple of weeks he was back at Conroy's side. Yet what happened on that day when the cloud of gas first found its way into the dog's lungs would forever change the terrier and his role.

Even though Conroy and others ordered him to stay in the trenches, now Stubby refused to obey them. No longer did he bark to encourage his companions, instead, he perched on the top of trenches, remaining silent, his eyes forward and his ears cocked. And only when he heard the sound of gas being released or smelled the odor accompanying that sound did he move. Suddenly, with no warning, he became a barking bundle of energy racing from trench to trench, an energized ball of fur seemingly intent on reaching every soldier in the area.

At first the men thought Stubby had finally succumbed to what they called battle fatigue. They assumed his injuries and the gassing had resulted in his going crazy. Thus they figured his days on the front were over. But soon Conroy understood. The dog recognized the gas before the men did. Through his nose and sharp ears, he sensed it. Suddenly the men had a warning system. Because of the dog they would have the time to slip on their gas masks and cover their exposed skin.

No longer was Stubby ordered back in the bottom on the trenches; the dog was now their sentry and leader. The men followed the canine's lead even more closely than they did their officer's commands. And why not? The dog was saving countless lives every day. Thanks to their canine advanced warning system, the 102nd's gas casualties were significantly reduced, and the company's ability to wage war on the enemy was much more effective.

In the quiet moments, when the battle was not raging, men began to seek out the little dog. They held him in their arms and whispered thanks into his ears. Some had tears in their eyes.

Stubby received treats along with praise and thanks. Some of the company's officers even began to salute the dog. If all he had done was to serve as an advance gas warning system, Stubby would have had more value than a hundred men. Yet, as the army would soon discover, this dog's battlefront education was about to open the door to his saving even more lives.

Perhaps because of his stays in field hospitals, Stubby also learned to listen for men in distress. Though no one ever understood how he distinguished between the enemy and members of his own military, the dog charged through fire and into no man's land when one of his own went down. He stayed by the wounded man's side until a medical team arrived. Sometimes that meant spending more than an hour in the midst of horrific fire from both sides. But his work as a medical spotter didn't stop there.

In the noise of fearsome battles, he somehow picked up on men who had been injured and fallen into trenches. He would jump into the trench with an injured man, bark nonstop until help arrived, and then race to the next victim. He even developed the ability to sense when a man was dead or alive. If there was no hope, he moved on to a soldier who was in need of aid and had a chance to survive. The medical core grew so amazed by the dog's instinct they tried to adopt him into their unit, but the 102nd would not give him up.

Stubby next developed the ability to hear the whine of artillery shells well before they could be picked up by human ears. More than that, he seemed to understand where the shells would land. Racing to that area, jumping up and down, and snarling, Stubby warned men to race from their positions and seek cover. As they did, the dog leaped into the bunkers with them. After the explosion he quickly emerged from the safety of the shelter and took up a post, sitting stone still, waiting until he heard the next shell coming.

Over the course of several months hundreds of men felt they owed their lives to the dog's warnings. Soon Stubby's companions held him in greater awe than they did General Pershing. As word filtered back to the States, families and even churches set aside time to pray for the little dog's continued service in the field.

One of the next skills that Stubby gained was first noticed by Conroy during a lull in a battle. The dog was unceasingly barking even though there were no signs of enemy action. No one could get him to quiet down. Frustrated, Conroy told the company commander about the dog's strange behavior. A few moments later sentries noted a group of Germans sneaking toward their lines for a night attack. Stubby's warning positioned the 102nd to be ready to confront the enemy and drive them back with no loss of life. After that, Conroy was told to report when the terrier seemingly went crazy for no reason. Each time it happened, it proved to be a warning of an approaching enemy.

Americans were engaged in almost hand-to-hand combat in the Argonne when Stubby stepped forward in a new capacity. Conroy was catching a nap in a foxhole when the dog jumped on his chest and began barking. Leaping to his feet, the soldier followed the dog through a maze of trenches to discover a German sniper who had infiltrated the American lines. Before Conroy could react, the dog sunk its teeth into the enemy's leg and clamped down. He didn't let go until the German threw down his gun and surrendered.

Frenchmen came to marvel at the dog that, in their minds,

defined courage, determination, and grit. As he proudly strolled through villages, men, women, and children clapped and cheered for the canine. Some even rushed forward with treats.

After retaking the town of Chateau-Thierry, the 102nd was given the chance to rest for a few days. During their stay in the city, a group of French women turned an army blanket into a small uniform. They presented this specially made jacket to the terrier. Conroy accepted the gift and put it on the dog. Stubby seemed genuinely proud to finally be wearing the colors of his company. Several of the men showed their great admiration by taking off their medals and pinning them on the new jacket.

In a year and a half of combat duty, Stubby participated in seventeen major battles including Chateau-Thierry, the Marne, and Saint-Mihiel. He also took part in four different offenses with his group, the 26th Yankee Division of the 102nd Infantry. As the days of the war wound down, officers ordered an official sergeant's jacket made for the canine hero, complete with his name. Pinned to that jacket were a Purple Heart, the Republic of France Grande War Medal, the Medal of Verdun, and ribbons and medals for every battle in which he participated. The wire services, which had briefly written about the dog a year before, now gave him the full hero treatment. Stubby's story of bravery found its way into almost every newspaper in the free world. By the time the armistice was signed, the once unwanted Boston terrier had become the most celebrated dog in American history.

Stubby had been smuggled to France and now, with the war over, an army rule stated that no dog, even if that canine was a decorated hero, could accompany the soldiers back home. Conroy went to several officers and all of them pointed to regulations and suggested the G.I. find a home for Stubby in France. Just like he had done when he left the United States for Europe, Conroy opted to smuggle the terrier back home. And this time the military police turned a blind eye allowing the dog and master to bend the rules.

Once back home, Stubby was greeted as a genuine war hero. The dog that had saved hundreds of American men was honored at scores of banquets and headed up many victory parades. The American Legion inducted him as a full, voting member. The YMCA offered him food for life. New York City's finest hotels welcomed him with free food and lodging.

Though the Army had cited rules as the reason he could not return to the States on a troop ship, with Stubby back on American soil they made an abrupt about-face and used the dog to recruit new men, sell victory bonds, and even lobby for funding from Congress. Stubby was invited to the White House and General "Black Jack" Pershing saluted the dog and pinned a medal on the canine's army jacket. The dog also found himself representing the Humane Society's goal for better treatment of animals and advocating for the Red Cross's blood drives.

When Conroy finally grew tired of the road, he and Stubby returned to Washington not as guests of the president, but so the man could attend Georgetown University Law School. As Conroy studied, Stubby hung out on the football field, getting to know the players, coaches, and cheerleaders and, because of his antics and tricks, was quickly adopted as the school's mascot. At halftime he entertained crowds by pushing a football all over the field. When the team raced back into gridiron for the second half, Stubby would stand and salute the men.

In 1926, Stubby's age, combined with the effects of his war

injuries, caught up with him. He no longer had energy in his step and it became an effort to stand and salute. He spent most of his time sleeping. One day he crawled up into Conroy's lap, and as the man petted his now graying head, the dog died.

Unlike many who fought in World War I, Stubby's death did not go unnoticed. Newspapers all around the country ran news of his passing. The nation's leading daily, *The New York Times*, cited an often-dismissed element of the dog's personality. The story the paper ran noted he was a cheerleader. He didn't just save lives; he lifted spirits, inspired courage, and led a charge to victory. In his obituary the *Times* closed with these thoughts, "The noise and strain that shattered the nerves of many of his comrades did not impair Stubby's spirits. Not because he was unconscious of danger. His angry howl while a battle raged and his mad canter from one part of the lines to another indicated realization." What the obituary writers missed was the dog's amazing determination to adapt and change. In every situation he was always looking to become more than what he had been and, over time, grew to become more than anyone could imagine.

America's devotion to Stubby was so great that the nation would not allow the war hero to simply be buried. They had this symbol of freedom and courage mounted and placed in an exhibit at the Smithsonian's Museum of American History. Yet the real monument to this dog's courage is not found at the Smithsonian; it can only be realized when imagining the hundreds of men who came home from World War I who otherwise would have—without this dog's actions—died on battlefields in France. Not a bad legacy for an unwanted pup that had once been turned out onto the streets to die.

4

POTENTIAL

★ ★ ★

LOOKING FOR A REASON TO LIVE

*I am here for a purpose and that purpose is to grow
into a mountain, not to shrink to a grain of sand. Henceforth
will I apply all my efforts to become the highest mountain of all
and I will strain my potential until it cries for mercy.*
—Og Mondino

In the canine world there is likely a bit of Lassie or Rin Tin Tin in every dog, but those who don't measure up to certain standards often never get an opportunity at life, much less a chance to make an impact and display the full measure of their worth. Eve's story is not one that will ever be made into a movie, and her face will never grace a sack of dog food. She didn't pull a human out of a flooding river, charge a mad cow to save a group of school kids, or drag a child down an ice-covered mountaintop to help and safety. Instead, Eve taught a simple but profound lesson in the meaning of acceptance, potential, and teamwork. That lesson should make us not only look at each dog differently, but every person as well. It also might cause us to redefine the word *hero* and rethink our definition of *trash*.

Eve's story began on December 24, 2012, a snowy day when there was hope in the air and anticipation around every corner. The traffic on the Tehachapi mountain roads around Bear Valley Springs, California, was heavier than usual as people made last-minute trips to stores for presents. The glowing faces of the children living in this natural paradise showed excitement and hope as they built snowmen and whispered of the upcoming visit of Santa Claus. Along the gated community's streets, decorations were draped from homes and the thin mountain air beckoned people inside for warm apple cider and homemade cookies. This was a Norman Rockwell Christmas come to life. Into this holiday postcard stepped a blond woman sporting a wide smile, cherry cheeks, and twinkling eyes even as she faced the busiest day of her year.

Six thousand feet above the valley over Bakersfield, California, in an area filled with huge ponderosa pines and century old oaks that framed views of desert vistas so far below, one of the postal service's finest, Molly, was bundled up to ward off the cold as she worked her way along the snow-covered Eve Deer Trail. Between shouting out greetings to friends, she hummed a holiday carol and marched forward with the enthusiasm of one of St. Nicholas's elves. While her workload on this morning might have been triple the norm and the short days made her job tough, she still loved every facet of the season. The cool air somehow warmed hearts with optimism, and the cards she delivered brought smiles and rekindled memories. It was a time of hope, life, and energy. It was day when bad news seemed to be forgotten as loving spirits took root and blossomed.

Molly was about halfway through her route when, stepping from her jeep, she heard a whimper that drew her eyes from the letter she was holding in her hand to a snowbank on her right. At first glance she saw nothing out of the ordinary. Still, the unusual noise caused her to pause for a moment before continuing her duties. Stepping forward, her boot crunching on the frozen ground, she heard the noise again. Stopping, she once more gazed into the drift. Shading her eyes from the glare, she finally spotted a puppy half buried in the snow.

If the pup did not die from exposure before sunset, it would become an easy meal for predators. And at night, when humans moved inside, the mountain came alive with bears, wolves, and even cougars. Molly could not allow that happen. As long as there was a chance it might live, she had to get help for the pup. Though tradition has it that letter carriers and canines are mortal enemies, on this day the letter carrier became an angel who moved forward and knelt on the cold ground. While stroking the puppy's tiny white head with her right hand, she dug out the snow around the animal with her left.

The pup looked to be about six to eight weeks old and was barely breathing. It was small, limp, and all but unresponsive. As it was bitterly cold, Molly pulled the tiny white creature into her arms and tried to warm it up. She was shocked when this simple act of kindness caused the puppy to stir and nuzzle her sleeve. Still, what do you do with a starving, dying pup on Christmas Eve? She had letters and packages to deliver and a thousand things on her own holiday list to accomplish after work, but they were all temporarily put on the back burner. This was Christmas and something greater was calling her, so she just couldn't leave the pup to die. And thanks to her duties with the postal service, she also knew there was a man a few miles away in Tehachapi who had devoted his life to saving dogs others didn't want. So, within an hour she was knocking on the front door of Zack Skow's log cabin.

Skow was an athletic man, a marathon runner with closely cropped hair and a chiseled jaw. His large expressive eyes lit up when he saw what Molly was cradling in the crook her of elbow. Reaching out, without hesitation he took the small, shivering puppy. He was still holding the tiny mass of fur when the letter carrier, satisfied she had done all she could do, wished the man a "Merry Christmas" and went back to work.

Four years before, Skow, a dog lover, founded Marley's Mutts. Inspired by a dog that he had been given, Skow made it his mission to take dogs out of kill kennels, then train and find them homes. For him this work was not a hobby; it was a calling. Using the three acres around his mountainside home, as well as depending upon friends who fostered animals for him, he had saved scores of dogs and united them with new families. Thus taking in an animal on Christmas Eve was almost as natural as decorating a tree or wrapping presents. But, as he would soon discover, this was no ordinary case. In fact, the pup Molly had given him would prove the licensed dog trainer's biggest challenge.

Almost lost in his big hands, the unexpected holiday gift whimpered a bit before curling up in a tiny ball. That small act of trust completely captured Skow's heart. Weighing only a couple of pounds, the animal was so undernourished its ribs were pushing through its coat and it was essentially more dead than alive. Still, its heart was weakly beating, and even if the puppy's life was now measured in just hours, Skow was bent on doing what he could to at least make this tiny white creature's last few moments a bit easier. And, as it was the day before Christmas, he immediately chose to name the puppy "Eve."

A quick examination convinced Skow that Eve was a purebred Catahoula Cur dog. They were also called leopard hounds and had been owned by the likes of some of the nation's greatest historical figures including Jim Bowie. Catahoula were a uniquely American breed with roots likely going back hundreds of years to Native American tribes. Though considered a hunting dog used to root out wild boar, the glassy-eyed animals were also employed in herding cattle. Outgoing, friendly, and great with children, they could grow up to seventy pounds. Though not one of the nation's most popular breeds, they were valuable and coveted by thousands of dog owners. So why had this one been dumped? It didn't take long for that question to be answered.

As Skow wrapped the puppy in a towel he discovered Eve was likely blind. One eye had never formed and the other was cloudy and small. Her teeth were also not as large as they should be. His experience told him the puppy had likely been her litter's runt.

Purebred dogs have to have a certain look. They must be strong, energetic, and handsome. They must be free of obvious flaws. Eve was none of those things and was therefore something a breeder could not sell. So rather than keep her around she was taken out into the mountain woods and thrown away. This heartless act fit in perfectly with the cruel standards of operations at puppy mills and with modern American life too. Two generations ago folks returned soda bottles to the store for deposits; now bottles, cans, and even food are tossed in the trash. In fact, Americans throw away more stuff than any nation in the world and this is even true of animals. Millions of pets are kicked out of homes every year because the owners don't have the patience to train them, the compassion to forgive their mistakes, or the character to overlook their flaws. Even sadder, pups that don't measure up to the standards set by breeders are often put down before they can even start to live. Eve was a product of the way things were, and she would have never had a chance to escape that cruel reality if not for a caring postal worker.

After getting some formula into the pup, Skow did a few more tests. What he discovered next caused his heart to sink even further. The dog appeared to be deaf too.

Skow was shocked that Eve made it through the night. Though small and weak, she seemed to have an oversized desire to live. And hour by hour and day by day, she fought her way back to health. But that was not enough to make this puppy a candidate for adoption from Marley's Mutts. She was handicapped, and in the dog world that was an even greater liability than in the human world. So, to get her into a loving home, Skow would have to devote more time and training to Eve than any dog that had ever come through his door.

By February, her initial brush with death behind her, she was physically strong and growing. Almost completely white with a few spots on her side, the short-haired dog with only slits for eyes had even become kind of cute, but her behavior issues likely meant she would never be a candidate for adoption. Not only was she scared of humans, her lack of social understanding caused the other dogs at Marley's to shun her. They treated her like a leper, and they had good reason.

Likely because she could not hear anything and only saw shadows out of one eye, Eve was paranoid and belligerent toward any dog or person that approached her. Possibly because of what she could barely see and not hear, when she was awake she barked unceasingly. She was so loud that it was impossible to even have a phone conversation if she was in the same room. Because she was deaf, Skow couldn't ask her to calm down and because she could barely see, he couldn't model behavior with hand signals. In a real sense, things seemed to be hopeless.

In an attempt to wear her out and get her to sleep, Skow took

Eve on runs. He found the dog was a natural athlete. She could race along the mountain trails for miles without ever becoming winded. In fact, she thrived on the exercise. She couldn't wait for the lead to be strapped on that signaled the start of her daily jogs. But as soon as they returned home and the leash was removed, the incessant barking began again. So did the aggressive behavior toward the other dogs. And if she got a whiff of a strange person in her domain, she really went crazy. Finally, the introduction of anything new into her world put her into a complete state of panic. Yet, in the face of overwhelming odds, Skow would not give up.

In early spring, through constant work, Eve began to make progress. She settled down to the point where the other dogs at Marley's could at least put up with her and she no longer went crazy when new people entered a room. She even toned down her barking. More important, thanks to Skow taking her places and exposing her to new people, she grew to be both gentle and trusting around humans. Still, even though his friends responded positively to Eve and grew to accept her handicap, would anyone ever want to adopt her?

Visitors stopped by Marley's Mutts on a regular basis to find a loving companion to bring into their families. But even though many came, not all got to leave with a dog. Because he so treasured the canines he had saved from being put down at animal shelters, Skow set high standards for the adoption process. Not everyone qualified, but those who did rarely bothered looking at Eve. Even though her manners were now acceptable, her physical problems were simply too intimidating. Therefore it shocked Skow when a couple finally asked about her. They had a child who also was suffering from a handicap and thought Eve might be a good match. After arranging a meeting, Skow believed the union of dog and family might just work. As Eve left to begin her new life, those at Marley's Mutts celebrated. The pup that had been tossed away like trash had now become an important member of a family and companion to a special needs child. This adoption fully validated Skow's work. But two months later it all fell apart.

With no warning Eve was returned to Marley Mutt's. The family that had adopted her now wanted nothing to do with the growing white pup. Once again Eve had been thrown away and if anything the scars this rejection created were even deeper than those inflicted on Christmas Eve.

Though she was fine physically, mentally Eve was a basket case. Skow discovered that during the two months she had been with the family, she had been kept in the backyard and literally ignored. She had rarely felt the touch of a human hand and had never been held. For a dog that could neither hear nor see, direct human contact was essential. Worse yet, all of Skow's work had been forgotten. Eve had lost all her social skills, trust of humans, and ability to mesh with other dogs. She was again scared of almost everyone and everything. When approached, she would growl and run. And, because she was blind, these panic attacks led to her charging into fences, chairs, and walls. She was also chasing imaginary creatures that only she could see. For hours she would run after things that were not there. It was as though she was haunted.

It took weeks for Skow to work back through the rash of new problems and begin to solve the old bad habits that Eve had again adopted. Though Eve slowly improved, Skow realized this dog would likely never leave his home. In fact, she was now such an outcast he doubted any other dog would ever have anything to do with her again. She seemed doomed to be a barking machine, a nuisance, and an insecure animal completely scared of the world and everything in it. In a sense, her life was a constant nightmare.

In the summer, as he continued to work with Eve, Skow got a called from a local boarding facility. A white mixed-breed, Dillon, had been left with them more than a year before and the owners had never come back to pick up the animal. If Marley's Mutts wouldn't take their unwanted guest, then the kennel was going to deposit him at the pound.

Dropping everything else, Skow drove down to Palmdale to meet Dillon. What he found was a scared, nervous dog that had no social skills. Unlike Eve whose breeding background was obvious, Dillon appeared to be part collie, part white German shepherd, and maybe a few other breeds as well. His big head, with its gray markings on the side just below the eye, gave him character. He was even cute in a Disney kind of way. His body was solid too. In the sports world, he would have been a linebacker. So, on the surface he appeared to be the kind of dog that would be fairly easy to place.

Yet, when Skow approached the fifty-pound animal and it growled and snapped, the picture changed. The dog trainer was then informed that not only was Dillon paranoid around people but he also rushed at other dogs. It seemed that all he really wanted was to be left completely alone in a place he considered safe, and in his mind, the real world—with all its strange sights, sounds, and smells—was to be feared. What could be causing this extreme antisocial behavior?

As Skow observed the dog pace in its enclosure, he soon discovered what was likely the root of the problem. Like Eve, Dillon suffered from some type of vision impairment. So added to his belligerent and aggressive behavior was a handicap. Figuring that Dillon could not be as much of a challenge as Eve, Skow loaded the dog into his car and took him to the vet. There it was discovered that not only was Dillon blind but he was also deaf.

Bringing the new dog home, Skow kept him on the lead and ushered him into the backyard so that he could be introduced to the other dogs. Dillon wanted nothing to do with any them. He was so filled with apprehension and fear that he tried to find a place to hide, but Skow's lead kept him in place. This made the dog's behavior even worse. When any of the curious dogs came close, he dug his feet in, snarled, and yowled. And then Eve came along.

Perhaps it was because she was deaf and almost blind, but she seemed to have no fear of the angry white-and-gray dog that was terrorizing the other six canines in the yard. Or perhaps, because she didn't get along with the other dogs either, Eve sensed she had something in common with the new arrival. For whatever reason, she was immediately curious about Dillon. As everyone waited for a fight to break out and Skow kept a tight grip on the larger dog's lead, Eve sidled up beside the new visitor and leaned her side into his. Rather than snap or run, Dillon remained perfectly still for a few moments and then opened his mouth, dropped his long tongue close to the ground, and grinned. For thirty seconds Eve leaned against the suddenly warm and friendly dog and then Eve led the way out into the yard. Dillon sprang up and followed. Within a minute, the two dogs, one almost completely blind and totally deaf, and the other sightless and deaf, were rolling beside each other in the yard. Then, with Eve leading the way, Dillon was introduced to his new world by a dog almost as blind as he was.

How had Eve sensed that Dillon needed her? She couldn't hear him and could barely see him. Thus she could not have observed that he was blind and deaf. So what pushed her to march up to a hostile dog and put her body gently against his? Where did this shy, confused dog find the courage to make that leap of faith? Eve was a dog that was scared of shadows and yet when all the other dogs backed away, she plunged into what could have been an explosive situation. It simply didn't make sense and is a mystery that no one has ever been able to explain.

Over the course of the next few days, the dogs became inseparable. They were each other's shadows sharing toys, treats, and hugs. Within a week their secure bond with each other led to their trusting and accepting the others dogs as well. With Dillon taking up all her waking hours, Eve even stopped her constant barking. So while Skow still didn't know if the two dogs could ever be adopted, they had at least found a way to fit in and enjoy the world. For animals that had been tossed away like trash and were dealing with severe handicaps, that in itself was a miracle. But more than just this, they were happy and carefree. They had even morphed into the yard comedians that made everyone who visited laugh at their antics.

As Skow considered the amazing transformation, he realized that Dillon had given Eve something she so desperately needed— a reason to live. Ever since the moment she was tossed into the snowbank, she had been fighting for life, but her life had very little meaning. Her greatest joy had come from running along mountain roads but that experience really had no purpose for her. Dillon had provided her with a calling in life. And having a sense of value gave her a reason to live and really enjoy life too.

Skow told his friends of the way Eve had immediately put Dillon at ease. He brought people to his home so they could observe the dogs' interactions. The guests marveled at the joy they witnessed as the two dogs played. As the full measure of what they observed hit them, it also sparked conversations of the value of life. Almost all of them left not only reevaluating the potential of special needs dogs, but of special needs people too.

Capturing video of Eve and Dillon, Skow shared their story on Marely's Mutts' website and the organization's Facebook page. Soon hosts of people were driving up the mountain to see the dynamic duo in person. One of those who made the trip was Shelly Scudder. In spite of preparing for a wedding, she took the time to come meet Eve and Dillon. They so capture her heart with their teamwork and fun attitudes, she stepped forward to adopt them as a pair. The dogs that no one wanted, the animals most felt should have been put down, now found a home where they could live together forever. The nightmare that had begun with a damaged pup being thrown away on Christmas Eve had been rewritten into a tale with a happily-ever-after ending that included a bride and her new groom and two special needs dogs becoming an instant family.

Eve's story might have started as nothing more than a special needs puppy being saved from dying in a snowbank, but the lesson of her life has grown into something that spotlights not just dogs, but people. In the human world, a hero is often a person who is athletic and beautiful. This is the type that almost always grabs the spotlight and becomes one of society's icons and role models. Yet there are people reaching out in small ways that make even more incredible impacts in the lessons they teach if not in the scope of their reach. In fact, there are heroes all around us who earn the title because they have the courage to accept others and see potential where most see none. They become heroic because they have the courage to take a leap of faith.

Eve was not considered worth even giving away. She was tossed aside like trash, all because she didn't measure up to the standards set by people who grade dogs on appearance and nothing else. The fact Eve was found at all was a Christmas miracle. Then the first time she was given a chance it was humans who let her down again. She came back to those who had worked with her with no hope of ever leaving the facility. Then she found her calling. That calling was to take another misunderstood dog under her wing. Dillon would have likely never gotten over his fear of the world without Eve. Eve would have never ridded herself of her antisocial behavior without Dillon. So Eve saved the life of another dog and saved her own as well. She found purpose and in the process fully adjusted to her handicaps. Eve's heroic actions define what breed standards can't see, much less measure, the potential of the encouraged heart. Through a step of faith, Eve proved that there was a bit of the Lassie and Rin Tin Tin in her, and, if you just look deep enough, there is a bit in probably every other dog too—even in the pups people throw away. In this case, one's man trash lived to become a great treasure of inspiration for canines and people alike.

5

DUTY

★ ★ ★

THE DOG TERRORISTS COULD NOT DEFEAT

I came to realize that life lived to help others is the only one that matters and that it is my duty.... This is my highest and best use as a human.
—Ben Stein

There are moments etched in time created by events that are too shocking for the human mind to fully comprehend. By dramatically reshaping history these incidents seem to stop time as well. They are never owned by a single individual, but are rather a collective moment that leaves a sharply focused imprint on every person that experiences them, no matter their age or station in life. They might be best defined as the moments "when everything changed."

If you go back in history two-hundred-forty years, that moment etched in time was April 19, 1775. It was defined as "The shot heard round the world." Thanks to that first blast of gunfire a revolution began. Though it took a while for the news to make its way to every part of the New World, it became a date deeply inscribed in the minds of people who would soon come to be called Americans. After all, it changed their world forever.

On April 12, 1861, more shots were fired and another war began at Fort Sumter, South Carolina. It was on this day the bloody Civil War tested the country's resolve for unity. For generations that spring date remained front and center in the minds of millions as the moment when a bloodbath began and when everything changed.

Eighty years later, on December 7, 1941, radios across America broke into regular Sunday programming with the news the Japanese had attacked the United States. In truth, many had no idea where Pearl Harbor was but they fully understood the uncertainty that lay ahead. They knew that because of that news today was much different than yesterday and there was no going back.

September 11, 2001, has a great deal in common with that trio of other riveting days in American history, but there is one exception that makes this event different. Those living in the country in 1775 knew that the colonists would eventually wage war against King George; the only question was when. The same held true for those anticipating the Civil War and World War II. Americans were going to war; those happened to be the moments that finally made that dreaded fact a reality. But no one could have guessed on that Tuesday in September that New York City and Washington, D.C., were going to be attacked. It was so far beyond the realm of thinking that a week after the horrific events many still couldn't believe the attacks had happened. But all they had to do was look around to see how much the events of one day had shaken a nation to its core.

Beyond the manner of the attack (a small band of men hijacking airplanes and using them as weapons), the fact it was the first strike by an outside force on the American mainland in almost two and a half centuries, and because of modern technology, 9/11 has been deeply imprinted into the minds of hundreds of millions. Never had history been so well documented. Almost from the beginning it was broadcast live. Americans didn't just hear about the events, they saw people die and watched buildings collapse. In an instant the country shuddered with a wave of insecurity and doubt that still affects us today. If ever there was a moment when everything changed, it was this one.

In all of the events that have been etched into history, heroes have arisen. They have led when others could barely move. They have shown resolve and courage. They have put others' needs ahead of their own. On September 11, 2001, many men and women found the courage to lead and inspire, and so did one yellow dog.

On that late summer morning, in the World Trade Center Tower 1, fifty-one-year-old Michael Hingson arrived early, unlocked the door to office suite 7827 and began setting up for a conference. He was in charge of the New York offices of Quantum/ATL, a data protection and network storage company. On this day he had an important meeting with six men from another firm that was interested in Quantum/ATL's services. While the jovial, fair-skinned man worked in his suit and tie, his constant companion, a yellow Labrador retriever, slept under his desk. The two-year-old dog's name was Roselle and she was a guide dog.

As he checked and rechecked the needs of his soon-to-arrive visitors, Hingson yawned. It had been an early morning. When a thunderstorm rolled into New York City it exposed once more Roselle's phobia of lightning and thunder. She was deathly scared of them. Thus, she had awakened her master early, even before the bad weather arrived, fretting about issues he could neither see nor do anything about. Hingson was both amused and frustrated that a dog that had no fear of walking the crowded streets of one of the world's largest and noisiest cities and would matter of factly fly in planes and ride in subways became a terrified puppy when confronted by a thunderstorm.

Blind almost since the moment of his birth, Hingson had been raised in Southern California by parents who treated him no differently than their sighted son. He was encouraged to always expand his horizons and leap over the world's conceptions of what someone without sight could accomplish. He was mainstreamed in school before that term was even recognized by the educational community and, by honing in on his other senses, he found his way around the school and community as well as most with 20/20 vision. After high school he went to college and then on to graduate school. As a student and then as a young man he was popular, outgoing, and a leader. He was so engaging that people often forgot the happy-go-lucky, charismatic soul was blind.

With guide dog in hand, Hingson began a career in computing and then sales. He traveled millions of miles in both the United States and around the world. He spent almost as much time in airports and on planes as he did at home. He only cut back on his almost nonstop schedule and embraced an office job when he got married. His drive and attitude paved the way for him to move up the ladder quickly and brought him to a station in life where the prestigious World Trade Center was his business address. As he began what he thought was just another normal day, he had no way of knowing that his being on the seventy-eighth floor of Tower 1 would lead to his dog helping to save lives in the midst of a nightmare few could even begin to imagine.

Though many think what guide dogs do is almost magical, nothing couldn't be farther from the truth. Like Roselle, these canine companions simply work as a team with their masters. It is not as much instinct as it is education that creates an animal that is trained to lead, protect, and serve. When on harness they are focused and driven to play out their roles, but off harness they once again become just another dog. On 9/11, Roselle would use that training and even, when challenged, go beyond.

At 8:46, Hingson was in the conference room when he and a coworker, David Frank, heard a tremendous explosion. A moment later the men felt the entire building dramatically lean to one side. Only by grabbing onto a table did they remain on their feet. Because of his California roots, the first thought in Hingson's mind was that it was an earthquake. And to shake a structure like the tower it had be a big one too. As the men held on for dear life, the building continued to lean, ceiling tiles started to fall, and chairs began rolling. Then, almost as soon as it had begun, the structure righted itself and all was once more seemingly quiet. But just beyond the building's outside walls, in a world Hingson could not see, things were now much different.

Frank walked over to the windows. He watched in disbelief as glass, paper, and debris flew past him and down toward the streets below. After filling Hingson in on what he was seeing, the two men decided it was in their best interest to evacuate. Six guests were waiting in the outer office and Hingson rushed out, informed the confused men some kind of accident had happened and that they should go to the stairwell and get out of the tower as quickly as possible. After the group left, Hingson hurried back into his office and was shocked to find the dog that had fretted over a small thunderstorm earlier that morning was still asleep under his desk. Only her master coming in the room had roused her from her slumber. She observed Michael shut down the computer systems and put files away before grabbing the harness and announcing, "Forward." With no hesitation, the guide dog went to work.

The floor's lobby was crowded. From every part of the room people were asking if anyone knew what had happened. Most figured it had been a fire, maybe a bomb, and some hinted at some kind of horrific accident. No one guessed that a fully loaded jet airliner, American Flight 11, had been purposely flown into the building's north side and had destroyed floors ninety-three to ninety-nine. At that moment, not knowing the truth was likely a good thing.

As people rushed to the stairwell, smoke began to fill the room, and Hingson had his first hint as to the cause of the explosion. He sensed something he had smelled at airports, but he couldn't put his finger on exactly what it was. At that very moment as much as 3,000 gallons of fuel was burning at over 2,000 degrees just ten floors above his head.

Roselle's first instinct was to lead Hingson to the elevator. That was their normal route when leaving the office. Yet the fact that smoke was indicative of a fire pushed the man on to the stairwell. Instincts combined with common sense led him to feel the safest escape was to walk down the seventy-eight floors rather than the normal and much faster method. As would be proven by those who had gotten into the elevators and died, his by-the-book judgment was spot on.

Another thing working in Hingson's favor and giving him confidence to trust the stairs was experience. He liked to explore. Even as a child he constantly pushed his boundaries and mapped out new areas of his world. In his time in the World Trade Center he had spent countless hours investigating the building with

Roselle. Hence, they were almost as familiar with the tower as the maintenance staff. So naturally, unlike many of the sighted people, the dog and the man had no problem finding stairwell B. With his friend Frank still at his side, and the dog leading the way, Hingson pushed out of the smoke and into the seemingly safe confines of the concrete, stair-filled chamber leading both up and down. There was no question which direction they were going.

At first navigating the nineteen steps between floors was not that difficult and they managed an almost normal pace working their way downward. But within a few floors hundreds of other refugees had joined them. Soon it was thousands and this massive convergence of confused workers and guests slowed their pace to a crawl.

For the sighted, claustrophobia often overrules reason. In the crowded conditions with movement all but slowed to a stop, with the temperatures rising and no one aware of what had caused this combustible situation, many were beginning to panic. Those trapped in the slow climb down the stairs were urging people forward, pleading with the line to keep moving, and even pushing a bit. Hingson could not only sense the crowd's fear, he could smell it. He was sure Roselle could as well. Reaching down he gently stroked the young dog's head, assuring her with his touch everything was all right. The Golden Lab didn't seem to need much comforting; she was as steady as a rock. It was hard to believe this was the same animal that was trembling a few hours before simply because of a bit of lightning and thunder. Suddenly Hingson sensed that Roselle's demeanor might serve a great use in the crowded stairwell. Finding his voice he explained the dog was so well trained, if there was any imminent danger she would let them know. As she was now so relaxed, there was nothing to fear. As they observed the dog, folks began to calm down. This was a kind of leadership that likely wasn't considered during her guide dog training, but thanks to that training her demeanor was taking the edge off a potentially volatile environment. A few seconds later, when the line started to move, Roselle again led the way.

As the long line of refugees inched downward, a woman voiced a concern that Hingson hadn't even considered. What would happen to them if the lights went out? How would they climb down in the dark? The blind man, his tone confident, once again chimed in, explaining that darkness was his native habitat and so it would be no problem. He and the dog could lead them out, lights or not.

They were almost halfway down when someone shouted for everyone to stop and move to the right. A few seconds later, four men carried a badly burned woman down the stairwell. After she had passed Hingson realized what he had first smelled back in his office. It was jet fuel. A plane must have flown into the tower. That explained everything including the woman's burns. Because something similar had happened at the Empire State Building in 1945, he figured it was likely nothing more than a tragic accident. And since the Trade Centers had been built to withstand such a disaster, firemen would no doubt soon have this episode under control. He would likely be back at work in a day or two. So now, as they again descended deeper down the stairwell, Hingson felt a sense of relief.

Roselle was panting deeply and had to be getting tired, but she didn't complain or even try to sit down. When she was given the chance, she moved forward, one step after another. And as the people around the dog watched her work, they seemed to gain courage and patience too. If the dog wasn't worried then there was no reason to be that concerned. Who would have thought a dog would have been the calming force during this bizarre ordeal?

Frank, Hingson, Roselle, and the others from floor seventy-eight were close to floor forty when the first fireman met them in their stairwell. One of the commanders even stopped to check on the refugees. He voiced great concerns about the blind man. He even offered to escort Hingson down to safety. Hingson assured him that thanks to Roselle he was far better off than anyone else. With a smile and wave, he convinced the fireman to continue on his way. He would never find out if the rescue worker made it out alive.

On the thirty-third floor a stairwell entry opened and a man handed out bottles of water. This simple act of charity buoyed the spirits of those slowly inching their way toward the main lobby. Even Roselle got the chance to quench her thirst. Moods remained high until a few minutes later when the lights suddenly went out. For everyone except the blind man the morning had become as black as midnight. People were scared and for some it felt as though the walls were closing in. This was the moment when panic seemed ready to overrule judgment.

"Nothing to worry about," Hingson assured them as he figured out what had happened. The blind man's words and ability to deal with the situation brought a sense of calm and a few seconds later the march to the lobby continued.

Making a step and then waiting was hard on the mind and the body. And, at the twentieth floor things became even more complicated and dangerous as water began to first leak and then almost pour into the stairwell. The building's sprinkler systems were waging a futile war to stop the fires. The liquid raced downward and into the stairwells making a continuous stream of waterfalls. Thus the footing was now unsure and people were leaning against the wall and each other to keep their balance. Yet, even in the dark while padding down wet steps, Roselle never stumbled. She kept moving and people kept following. Fifteen very long minutes later, those who had ducked into the stairwell on the seventy-eighth floor were finally at the lobby. Buoyed by a great rush of hope they emerged from the darkness and into the light. They were greeted not by open arms and a sense of great hope, but by absolute chaos.

People were running everywhere. First responders were racing in from the streets as building workers rushed out. Chairs had been knocked over, glass was broken, and people were screaming. Policemen were encouraging the crowd to keep moving, but some were seemingly frozen, their eyes locked onto images they couldn't quite believe. It was a mix of bedlam usually only found in Hollywood disaster films, but in this case the drama was real. Amid all the confusion and panic, Roselle tranquilly waited. Maybe better than anyone on that day, she fully grasped the only thing to fear was fear itself and she felt none.

As people dashed in every direction, Frank leaned over to Hingson and said, "We need to get out of here." Roselle instantly moved forward, guiding Hingson around furniture and panicked building employees while occasionally stopping to allow policemen and firemen to pass. When they finally made it out into the street they were greeted by a gaggle of reporters wanting to know what they had seen. As witnesses shared what they knew, Hingson finally learned what had actually happened. This had been a terrorist attack. The planes had been used as weapons. Both towers were on fire, and hundreds or perhaps thousands had died. The news was so sobering he could barely comprehend what it meant. Why would someone do this? What could be the purpose? Now, with the full toll of the disaster setting in, he realized he had someone he had to reach.

Ordering Roselle to stop, Hingson pulled out his cell phone and tried to call his wife. He couldn't get a signal. As he hit redial, Frank gave his friend a blow by blow of what he was seeing. Both buildings were on fire, people were leaping from the top floors to keep from being burned alive, huge chunks of concrete and large pieces of steel framing littered the ground and broken glass was everywhere. And then, at 9:59, came that horrible sound. Far from being over, this nightmare was just beginning.

Hingson felt the urge to cover his ears to try to muffle the long, growing rumble that sounded like a hundred tornados striking at once. The ground shook, Tower 2 groaned, people screamed, and a curtain of debris fell. Then the building started to collapse.

"Run," Frank yelled not bothering to explain why.

Hingson didn't have to be asked twice. The blind man had no idea what was in front of him, he simply had to trust the dog to guide him safely along a sidewalk filled with frightened masses trying to escape the same horror that was chasing him as well. Giving Roselle the order, they raced forward.

Though he could not see the cloud of dust that quickly enveloped them, Hingson could feel it coating his hair, face, and body.

It was sticking to his lips, invading his mouth, and pushing into his throat. He could barely breathe and had no idea what was in his path or who was around him. And, without any urging, Roselle kept moving.

The long walk down the stairwell was just an extension of the training Roselle had received in guide dog school. The patience she exhibited was also a part of that training. So, except for the heat, smell, and crowded conditions, there was nothing unusual about the experience inside the building. She had simply done what a guide dog was supposed to do. But this new dynamic made everything different.

As she turned onto Front Street she likely could see nothing while the sounds of Tower 2 falling were still echoing in her ears. Behind her, lapping her heels, was a war zone filled with scared and confused people and tons of debris. Screams were coming at her from every direction. People were crying for help. She was breathing dust, and her eyes and nose were caked over. She was pulling her master through a scene of absolute pandemonium. No training could have prepared her for this, and every natural instinct demanded she run away as fast as she could to safety. Yet her sense of duty kept pushing her forward. Though she couldn't understand the concept of Hingson not being able to see, she still somehow knew that without her leading the way this man would be lost. She and he were a team, and that team was going to either live together or die together.

Behind her, Hingson was covering his mouth and trying to catch his breath. Yet he wasn't thinking only of himself. He had so much faith in the dog that was now guiding him blindly through the New York streets that he latched on to others and urged them to follow. Those who had stopped in shock, frozen in place and so overcome by bewilderment they had given up, awoke with new hope. No longer was Roselle just leading Hingson, now there were many following behind her.

If he had not been caught in the drive to survive, Hingson might have stopped and marveled at his dog's incredible fortitude. Nothing was going to stop her. Even the sirens and screams were not going to slow her down. She had to get him to a place he would feel secure. What an amazing dog she was! This guide dog for the blind had become a guide dog for everyone.

A voice called out through the dust begging those running to come inside. Hingson pushed Roselle right and then trusted her to guide him to that friendly voice. The others following behind the dog fell in place as well. A few moments later a door opened and half a dozen refugees rushed in.

Hingson wanted to get as far into the building as possible. Everything in his being yelled at him to hurriedly move forward and race into the unknown. But just after they entered, Roselle stopped and would not move. Even as others pushed from behind, the dog held its ground. Few realized this was a subway entrance. Though covered with dust, panting deeply and barely able to see, the dog would not allow anyone to charge forward because doing so meant plunging down the stairs. This simple act, so essential in guide dog training, likely saved several, including Hingson, from severe injuries or death. So not only did she lead them to safety, she kept them safe once they arrived.

It took a full day for Hingson and Roselle to make it home. The still dust-covered man was exhausted and worn out when he finally felt his wife's arms around his neck. As they hugged and cried, Roselle, now no longer on harness and not needed to guide her master, picked up a toy and begged to play. Though terrorists had brought down both World Trade Center Towers and damaged the Pentagon, though they had shaken the country and its people to the core, the simple act of being ready to play proved they couldn't phase or defeat Roselle. Her response during the moments after tragedy reflected her incredible training, and her reaction when she arrived home foreshadowed the will and determination of the people of the United States to not let the violent and evil acts of this day quash the American dream or way of life.

Roselle would live another decade, but her service as guide dog was cut short due to health issues likely caused by the dust she inhaled as she led Michael Hingson out of the cloud of debris. Still, even though she was no longer leading her master, her career was far from over. In the years after 9/11, she appeared on a wide variety of television talk shows and became the living symbol of the value of service dogs. During that time, his priorities deeply changed by what he experienced in Tower 1, Hingson left the business world and became a powerful spokesman for employing people with disabilities.

The much-honored yellow lab's story and her master's inspiring life and message are spotlighted in the bestselling book *Thunderdog*.

6

FORTITUDE

★ ★ ★

THE WILL TO FINISH THE CLIMB

There are three things in life you need: fortitude, tenacity, and guts. Fortitude to stand no matter what, tenacity to stick with it, and guts to deal with whatever is in front of you.
—*Unknown*

The passing of one year to the next is usually seen as more than just the turning of the calendar, it is an opportunity to compose a new chapter in the book of life. It is a time of faith, second chances, and great optimism. Even on the coldest early January day there is still the warm lure of hope that drives men, women, and children to make resolutions and believe in dreams. In those first few days of a new year, thoughts of death are pushed aside and life is pursued as if there are an endless number of tomorrows. Yet especially on these often unpredictable winter days, the line between life and death is often as thin as the ice on a rural pond. As he bounced out of bed on a bright Saturday morning, little did a buoyant Michael Miller realize that he would soon be facing death, alone except for his shadow.

Only a couple hundred people call Bethpage, Tennessee, home. A rural community located just a stone's throw from Kentucky, Bethpage is one of those increasingly rare places where doors are often left unlocked and everyone is on a first-name basis. In 1998, life in this tiny community was much the same as it had been fifty years before. It revolved around churches and school, as well fishing, hunting, and quilting. A perfect weekend was more often spent enjoying nature than playing video games or making the hour-long drive down U.S. Highway 231 to

Nashville. And on this cold winter's morning it was the lure of the hunt that called most strongly to thirty-six-year-old Miller.

Living in the wooded countryside, the good-looking, broad-shouldered, rugged Miller owned land that was a sportsman's paradise. A combination of fields, streams, and trees provided natural homes for a wide variety of wildlife. On this winter's morning, the cloudless sky, the light wind, and the freezing temperature signaled the perfect day for hunting doves. A gleam showed in the man's sharp eyes as he stepped off the front porch, squinted into the morning sun, and headed up a hill with his dog, Sadie, happily leading the way.

Sadie, a forty-five pound English setter, was one of those lucky dogs that had the perfect master. Like Miller, she loved running through the forest and across fields. Nature was as much her passion as it was his. Every day offered a new world filled with yet undiscovered wonders. When alone, driven by curiosity as much as instinct, her nose always to the ground, her dark brown eyes focused on everything from soaring hawks to scampering rabbits, her white and brown body was alive with action. But when she was with Miller, her training took over. Then her solitary focus was a goal and that goal was uncovering prey.

For more than four centuries English setters like Sadie have been pointing out winged game to hunters. The breed was developed at the time when the British moved from arrows to guns. Trained to not only find and flush the birds but also to stay calm during the firearm's discharge, the English setter is a canine with a singular purpose. And because of that purpose, few members of the breed are seen outside of rural areas. But folks around Bethpage knew Sadie's name and recognized what an outstanding animal she was. Many of Miller's friends would have paid well to have her lead them during their hunts, so he considered himself a lucky man to have the canine as not only his companion during the hunts but also his shadow in life.

Setters are by nature high-energy animals. They love to run, and when not hunting, they are carefree children of the dog world. They have little desire to herd sheep or do farm chores, they don't pull wagons or sleds; for them, life is a play just waiting to be experienced. Therefore, nothing in Sadie's breeding or training positioned her for the responsibility that was about to fall on her slight shoulders and lean body. This is what makes her story all the more remarkable and makes the fact that Michael Miller is still alive a miracle.

Since he could walk, Miller was fascinated by the almost hidden activity that was ripe in the woods. In truth, finding doves was a secondary reason to his being outdoors on this Saturday morning. He relished each moment spent in the midst of beautiful, unspoiled nature. It was an experience he treasured almost as much as life itself. In fact, he had spent so much time in the outdoors his keen eyes easily spotted many things others missed. He noted all but hidden bird nests, the almost silent movement of a small group of deer, the light scampering of a pair of squirrels up a tree, and the tracks of larger animals pushed into damp sod. Thus the forest was a place of wonder and grace, majesty and power, and solitude and introspection. And unlike in the traffic jams he had fought from time to time in the big city, in nature he felt a sense of control. Here he had the needed skills to take on whatever confronted him and handle it by himself. Thus, alone in nature it was as if he was the ruler of his domain, and his power knew no bounds.

Miller had planned only a short hunt on this Saturday. He had too many things to do back home to make a day of it. Yet as the morning sun sparkled off frosted fields, Miller knew it was going to be tough giving up and heading back to the house. The crisp air brought him alive, giving him an energy that beckoned him deeper into the woods. Even if he and Sadie came home without any birds, this had the promise of a day that should not be missed. It was, in his mind, a bit of heaven on earth.

As the sunlight filtered through the bare limbs of a hickory tree, the hunter's attention was drawn to Sadie nosing around just ahead. That was the instant he barely noticed the first slight twinge of pain in his arm. He figured it was a cramp from carrying the gun, so he shifted the weapon to the other side. A few seconds later the aggravating sensation grew slightly worse, but Miller still reasoned that it was nothing to worry about and it would pass as quickly as it came. He figured it as likely nothing more than a slightly pinched nerve.

Moving forward, trying to ignore the tightness now moving to his right shoulder, he turned his attention to Sadie. Even though they were only a third of a mile from home, she looked as if she was on to something. Her nose to the ground, she was anxiously pushing a bit farther down the hill toward a meadow. No doubt about it, she had found game.

Cradling his gun in the crook on his left arm, Miller used his left hand to rub his right arm. As he did, he glanced back over toward the house. It was no longer visible, hidden behind the crest of the hill they had crossed a few minutes before. As Sadie moved farther away from him, he considered turning back toward home, but that thought was immediately wiped from his mind and replaced with an electrifying agony far beyond any he had ever known.

The once slight tightness in his arm now raced through his body like a bolt of lightning. In an instant the pain had become searing, pushing through his ribs and deep into his chest. His eyes still locked on the hilltop, Miller now realized something was incredibly wrong. Grunting, a confused expression framing his face, his gun dropped from his hand as he wrapped his arms around his chest and awkwardly fell to his knees. His face ashen white, the beautiful world around him now barely visible, Miller thought for a second of his wife, so close, yet so far away. Instinct told him to scream out to her, but logic dictated that she would never hear his cries. Still, he had to try something! Then, as if hit by a heavyweight champion's long right hook, he sank to his knees and fell to the cold ground.

Miller was slim and muscled. He was in great shape, a man of self-discipline and no bad habits. He was not under stress. Nothing in his family background forewarned of what had just happened. But nevertheless he knew what was going on. Just like it had been placed in a blacksmith's vise, a force that could not be seen was squeezing the life from his toned body by restricting every movement of his heart. It felt as though it would burst. He didn't have a cellphone and was too weak to even cry out for help. He was just over 1,700 feet from his front door but it might as well have been a hundred miles. In an act fueled by both panic and desperation, he tried to muster the strength to rise from the ground, but he couldn't.

Sadie was so immersed in her job she had not yet noticed her hunting partner was no longer following along behind her. Even as he writhed on the ground, she moved farther and farther away, her complete attention on the doves she knew were just ahead. Behind her a desperate man was fighting for his life.

A few minutes before, he was lord of his world and now he was alone and powerless and growing weaker by the second. Miller knew his fate was in his hands alone. He had to get up and fight his way back home to get help. So he tried to rise but failed to lift his stomach off the cold, damp ground. He was as helpless as a newborn child. If only he had told his wife, Lisa, which way he was going. If only he had asked her to come looking for him if he didn't show up back home soon. But his treks in the woods often lasted for hours, so it would be afternoon before she became worried. The only way for him to get the help he needed was to somehow get back to the house. And how could a man who couldn't even turn over or raise his voice above a whisper do that? As the pain continued to rip through his chest, he pushed himself to focus on his options. If Sadie were like TV's Lassie, he'd simply call her to his side, explain the situation, and ask her to go get help. But Sadie was no Lassie, in fact, she was still wandering in the woods looking for birds, completely unaware he needed her help. He'd likely be unconscious or even dead before she returned.

Once again Miller tried to find the strength to at least rise to his knees. Yet calling upon every bit of the athletic reserve in his body proved fruitless. He was all but paralyzed, so weakened by what he now felt sure was a heart attack that he could not even manage audible speech. Still, his mind was working well enough for him to know if he didn't find the strength to crawl back home, he was probably going to die.

As tears clouded his eyes, Miller remembered the dog whistle hanging from his neck. He used it to let Sadie know when he needed her to come back to his side. It was often the only thing that kept the dog from wandering too far away from the man. His hands shaking, the camouflage-clad sportsman grabbed for the whistle. Trying to ignore the pain and calm his ragged breathing, Miller shoved the brass instrument between his lips. His strength almost depleted, his mind beginning to drift into a semiconscious state, he weakly pushed his breath through the whistle. He blew several times, each toot robbing him of what little energy remained in his body. Then, without knowing if Sadie had heard his efforts, the man's head sank down onto the frozen ground.

It had only been a minute since the first burst of agony had ripped through his body, but it seemed like a lifetime. Now, after trying to call Sadie back to his side, Miller found himself sliding into a foggy world that made little sense. It was as if his body was racing to die while everything around him was moving in slow motion. Lifting his chin, he breathed a silent prayer and tried to focus on the horizon as his pounding heart strove to rip his ribcage to pieces.

Somewhere in the back of his mind, Michael heard what sounded like an animal running across dry grass and leaves. Was it a deer, a coyote, or maybe a wild dog? Lifting his eyes, he was comforted when he spied familiar white paws racing up to him. Sadie had heard the whistle and come back to his side.

Seeing her master flat on the ground must have initially confused the dog. She had to be wondering what kind of new game he was playing. Was this part of a training drill? Did he want to wrestle? Yet as the seconds ticked by, as she observed his moans and saw the tears stream down his cheeks, her playful expression was transformed into a look of genuine concern. Lowering her head to lick away a salty teardrop, Sadie quietly cried out. Suddenly there was hope, if Miller could somehow get Sadie to keep mournfully baying then perhaps Lisa would hear and come to his rescue. Yet, after her initial moan, Sadie remained mute and Miller didn't have enough strength to coax anything more than a soft whimper from his companion. So he had to come up with something else.

If he could convince Sadie to go home and if Lisa saw the dog without him, then maybe she might wonder what happened and come looking for him. Yet in spite of all the training he'd given the setter over the years there was no command for Sadie to go home. He had never taught her one. So even if begged her to go get Lisa, the dog wouldn't understand what to do. He had taught her so much, she was so loyal, and yet one simple lesson that he'd neglected now would likely cost him his life. Besides, Sadie was his shadow, and as she now sensed something was wrong, she was not going to leave him.

As Sadie continued to cry and lick his face, Miller reached up a few inches and patted her head. This simple act seemed to help ease the pain. Maybe he could find the strength to make it home after all. With a new sense of hope and Sadie's barks encouraging his every effort, Miller tried to stand. He fell and tried again with the same result. And with each new attempt, the pain raging in his chest grew worse. After several minutes of giving more effort than he had expended in his entire life, the strong 180-pounder couldn't even rise to his knees. Knowing what little hope he had was ebbing away, Michael grabbed onto Sadie's collar with his right hand and tried to use the dog's neck as leverage. Again he failed to stand. Crying, his tears streaming down his face to the ground, his hand slipped from the dog and back to the ground. All there was to do now was wait for death. How he hated for Lisa to find him this way.

Lying on his stomach, his cheek resting on the cold ground, Miller sought out Sadie. He wanted to touch her. At least one more time he needed to hold onto her and feel the presence of the animal that so dearly loved him. As he whispered her name, she instantly returned to his side.

When Miller's hands curled around Sadie's leather collar, he was resigned to dying in the woods with his hands on the best dog he'd ever known. At least now he wouldn't face the end alone. As he fought the cold and the pain, he wondered how long the brown-and-white canine would stay beside him after he'd taken his last breath. He figured she would remain until they found him. In that way she would be his shadow to the bitter end.

A sad expression in her deep eyes, she now finally understood that this was no game. Her master was not just taking a nap. Faced with this new situation, a host of conflicting instincts must have been crowding into her mind. After several moments of lying beside him, his hand locked onto her collar, the setter dug her paws in the soil and made an effort to move up the hill and in the process yanked Miller a few inches across the frozen grass.

Sadie weighed just forty-five pounds. She was not bred nor trained to pull anything. Yet some instinct, perhaps going back hundreds of years, kicked in. She was suddenly determined to take Michael home a few inches at a time.

Half crouching, she pushed her shoulders forward and took another step. She was not getting any kind of footing in the hard, frozen ground, but Sadie still managed to drag Miller a few inches with each of her gritty steps.

Miller's mind was now so clouded and confused he didn't fully comprehend what his dog was attempting to do. He just didn't want to lose touch with Sadie, so he kept his fingers curled around the collar and let her slowly drag him. Ten yards became twenty and the distance to the top of the rise grew closer. Twenty more minutes, and they were a hundred yards up the hill. Sadie took a deep breath, rested for a few seconds, took another look at the hilltop, and dug back in, bravely putting one foot forward and then another. Growing tired, she slipped to her knees, but rather than quit, she got up, and continued to move ever closer to home.

Slipping in and out of consciousness, Miller's lips were now blue and his skin pale. Those moments he could focus he stared at Sadie's face. She was determined and resolute. She'd somehow realized she was his only hope and she was going to drag him home even if it killed her.

Each foot of the journey was as painful for the man as it was the dog. The same rocks and limbs that were causing Sadie to lose her footing and slicing her paw pads were raking across his body creating bruises and cuts. Yet they were headed home, so pain began to diminish as hope once again took root in Miller's heart.

Crying as she pulled, Sadie covered a third of the distance in just over a half hour. She was exhausted, her tongue all but dragging the ground. Yet rather than give up to stop and rest, she lowered her shoulders and dug her paws in deeper. Gamely she pushed on, constantly checking the distance to her destination as well the expression on Miller's face.

"Good girl," he whispered so softly he didn't know if even Sadie's sharp ears could hear him. "Keep going, girl," he begged as she dragged him yard after yard.

If Sadie heard Miller, she likely didn't understand what he was saying. For the moment she was no longer a hunting dog, she was a canine SUV intent on conquering 1,700 feet a few inches at a time. She was of a singular mind—something was wrong and she needed to get her master home.

As she crested the hill, Sadie must have sensed the worst was behind her. Pulling Miller downhill was much easier than the first two-thirds of the trip, but as tired as the dog was, each step was still a monumental effort. Sadie's muscles were aching, her heart pounding so loudly that even groggy Miller could hear it. Now Miller began to wonder if the dog could manage the last few steps of the way. Was she actually going to give her life so that he might have a chance to live?

It took the setter just over an hour to complete her impossible journey and drag the man who outweighed her by one-hundred-forty pounds into the yard. Now, just as some deep-seated instinct had told Sadie to pull Miller the third of a mile to home, another instinct told the dog to fight free of the man's grip. Shaking loose, she raced to the back door, yelping and scratching until Lisa came to find out what was the fuss was all about.

"Sadie," the woman scolded, "you know better than that. Quit it."

Yet the normally well-behaved dog wouldn't stop. Instead, as if possessed, she charged up to the woman, then turned and ran a few feet into the backyard.

"Sadie," Lisa practically yelled, "what has gotten into you? I'm going to put you in your pen until you can calm—"

Lisa never finished her threat as her eyes fell upon her husband's crumpled and motionless form just a few yards in front of her. "My Lord," she sighed, rushing out the door. Lisa and Sadie both arrived by the man's side at the same time.

For a few moments Lisa tried to rouse her husband. It was a useless effort. He was now completely unconscious, much closer to death than life.

"Stay with him, Sadie," Lisa ordered as she ran back to the house. Grabbing the phone, the woman dialed 9-1-1. Then Lisa and the dog tried to comfort Miller and each other as they waited for the ambulance.

Within twenty minutes paramedics were ministering to the barely breathing man. Doing all they could for him on site, the medical team then raced him to Nashville's Saint Thomas Heart Institute. In the emergency room, Miller was stabilized and prepared for emergency triple bypass surgery. The next few hours would be the longest of Lisa Miller's life, yet somehow her husband fought off not just the extensive damage to his heart but also the numbing cold and injuries he'd experienced as the noble English setter had dragged him home.

For more than a week, Sadie waited, not knowing what had happened or if she would ever see her master again. During those long days she ceased running joyfully through the woods and wouldn't touch her food. Then, on a sunny day not unlike the one eight days before when the adventure had started, the family car drove up and Michael Miller got out. The setter's face showed her great joy, yet somehow sensing Miller was still weak, she approached him cautiously. Though Lisa begged her husband to go immediately inside and rest, the man took a moment and leaned down to thank the dog that had given him a second chance at life. As the two looked into each other's eyes, the bond that had held them together for a third of a mile more than a week before was cemented again.

"I certainly would have died in those woods if Sadie had not been with me," Miller explained to the local media. "I could have never made it on my own, and it's amazing that she was able to drag me back to the house."

The almost fatal heart attack and the heroic actions that saved Miller's life were just the beginning of the story. Over the next few months, it was walks in the woods, surrounded by the natural beauty he loved, that helped the man regain his strength. Always by his side, always there in case she was needed, Sadie shadowed his every step, ready to not only save a life but also to make living a great deal richer.

It has long been said that courage is not displayed when you do what you are trained to do, but is found when you do the unexpected. Sadie proved the size of her heart and the full measure of her devotion by stepping beyond what she should have been able to do and doing the impossible.

7

LOYALTY

★ ★ ★

IT'S THE SIZE OF THE HEART THAT MATTERS MOST

Where the battle rages, there the loyalty of the soldier is proved.
—Elizabeth Rundle Charles, sometimes attributed to
Martin Luther

She was the most unlikely of all World War II heroes. She weighed just over four pounds, had a soprano yelp, and a knack for getting into trouble. Curious, energetic, and smaller than many of the rats that American soldiers, sailors, and marines found in the Pacific Theater, Smoky should have been nothing more than a canine comedian providing laughs during the moments between battles. But, thanks to grit, enthusiasm, and intelligence, the diminutive Yorkie became a champion. Even today, more than seven decades after her service with the Army Air Corps, Smoky is still remembered and written about. In fact, the little dog with the big heart even has a Facebook page, a two-ton statue celebrating her remarkable life, a biography and, as recently as 2012, was honored by an Australian hospital.

She was near death when Pennsylvania native Army Private Bill Wynne, the man whose life she would save and future she would dramatically alter, was first introduced to the tiny bundle of fur. In early spring of 1944, Wynne, who worked with the Air Corps photography division, was stationed in Nadzab, New Guinea. He was on his way to a canvas field laboratory used for developing negatives and making prints when he spotted the pup tied to a tire. Underfed and weak, the grayish-gold animal was also starving for attention. Whenever a visitor walked in she would spin around, yelp, and beg to be petted. Wynne, who, in his youth, had owned and trained a number of mutts, was completely taken by the little dog's spunk and energy. Grinning, he picked her up and turned the pup over in his hands. What he found caused his heart to sink.

It was obvious that whoever owned the diminutive critter was not doing a good job with her care. The flea-covered Yorkie's ribs were almost protruding through her matted fur. She was not just dirty and starving, she was also dehydrated. If immediate action was not taken, the dog would likely die.

Wynne was a man whose military duties often required him to be a powerless passenger while flying into some of the toughest places of the Pacific front. Camera in hand and peering into active war zones, he shot photographs used by American intelligence to gauge enemy strength and plan attacks. Each day he went up in a plane, he knew all too well that the Japanese were on his tail. And because he was shooting film and not bullets and had to rely on someone else to fly the plane and get him home, his fate was always in the pilot's hands. Therefore, in the case of the dog, he just couldn't walk away and leave her care to someone else.

Asking around the tent and the company motor pool, Wynne finally found the person who had claimed the pooch as his own. The gabby sergeant explained the dog had been found trapped in a foxhole along the side of jungle road. If it hadn't been for a Jeep stalling out, it would have never been seen. The driver heard its cries, jumped into the trench, picked it up, and tossed it into the vehicle. When he came back to their camp the soldier dropped it off at the photo pool. In other words, it was just a stray, but as possession was nine-tenths of the law, the sergeant explained that if Wynne wanted it, the mutt would cost about five bucks.

Initially the photographer passed on the offer but another boring night in his jungle tent caused him to rethink the purchase. Though he had to be ready on a moment's notice to hop in a plane and shoot photos of installations, battles, ship formations, and supply lines, there were many times when he waited days between assignments. During this down period he played baseball, cards, and read, but now those activities were boring. On top of that the oppressive heat and humidity zapped his vitality and spirit and made him even more homesick. He therefore needed a diversion, and the dog needed someone who could nurse her back to health. Thus, this chance meeting between man and beast appeared to a prescription for a bit of happiness in the hell that was war. After an early morning trip back to the photo tent and an exchange of money, the dog had a new home in a high-roofed tent on a hill overlooking a vine-covered jungle.

Dogs in combat zones were not uncommon. Beyond the canines trained by the military for a wide variety of duties, many military units found and kept stray mutts as mascots. But few of these dogs were the product of careful breeding. Wynne's charge was a Yorkie, and during the 1940s the Yorkshire terrier was not a common breed. Even seeing a dog like this in Wynne's current hometown of Cleveland would have been unusual, and having a tiny dog with royal lineage left in a jungle foxhole was simply mind-boggling. So how had a dog the size of one of the soldiers' combat boots gotten lost in the New Guinea jungle? There couldn't have been a breeder within five hundred miles. This was not the kind of pooch Japanese soldiers or local natives would have purchased and brought into this hostile environment. So where did she come from? The question would haunt Wynne for years.

Due to her coloring, the American photographer named the Yorkie "Smoky" and nursed her back to health by sharing both his devotion and rations. And while Wynne had long ago grown tired of eating the same bland meals every day, Smoky had no aversion to army chow. She thrived on it, quickly doubling her size to her peak weight of four pounds. With this growth came amazing energy. The yelping little dog was never quiet and she was small enough to get into everything from trash pits to ammo dumps. In a very real sense, because of her size and antics, Smoky quickly became a dose of happiness and that was something this remote camp rarely experienced.

While the C-rations seemed the perfect dog food for the minute pooch, the conditions in the jungle were anything but ideal. The heat and humidity were hard on the pup. So were the ticks, fleas, and a myriad of other local parasites. Thus, Wynne was forced into a daily ritual of bathing the dog. Her bathtub was his army helmet and, due to this amusing marriage of military hat and a toy canine, bath time became a favorite spectator sport at the camp. Watching a full-grown dog whose body could completely disappear in a helmet became a welcome diversion, a great photo opportunity, and a topic that headlined many men's letters back to the States.

Beyond the heat, the environmental element that worried Wynne even more than Japanese attacks were the snakes. There were pythons all around them and they often crawled into tents at night searching for food. Smoky was a perfect size snack for one of these slinking predators, so Wynne had to come up with a plan to keep her safe. As he couldn't prevent the snakes from coming under the canvas walls, he created a suspended bed for the dog. Made from a canvas bag, Smoky would use this bed for the remainder of the war. And, as fate would have it, this World War II version of a carry-on bag would serve the dog on land, sea, and in the air.

One of the things Wynne grew to dislike was being stuck in camp for days at a time between missions. During these periods he had little to do but clean cameras and print photos. With Smoky he at least had a constant companion during those long days. Because of this time together, the bond between them was quickly cemented. While the dog might have liked everyone in the camp, it was obvious her true devotion was marked for one person.

Once she was fully healthy, the army photographer began teaching the dog tricks. When she quickly mastered the basics of sit, stay, and heel, he moved on to higher education. Fetch was no issue as long as he used a small ball; neither was begging, playing dead, or walking on her back legs. Her learning curve moved up so quickly it became a mighty task to come up with new ways to challenge her. Within weeks the Yorkie was even walking on a rolling barrel and balancing on tightropes. She also learned one more very important skill. When the sirens rang out the warning for Japanese air raids, Smoky raced to the bomb shelter.

Hiding in a hole while bombs dropped all around the camp unnerved a lot of the men. Some grew so scared of being buried under the ground due to an explosion they refused to go down in the shelters. Over the next few months, the dog was forced to seek shelter more than a hundred times. When she and Wynne came out they were often greeted by a far different world than they had left. Tents and equipment had been destroyed and friends were wounded or dead. The dog grew used to watching her master help others clean up and rebuild. Sometimes they had barely started this task when the sirens sounded again.

Even Smoky, who often barked unceasingly during her playful moments, remained mute during the raids. Yet having the little dog in the shelter seemed to bring a calming effect to this life-and-death situation. Perhaps because Smoky never got hurt in an attack, many soldiers saw it as a sign that she knew where it was the safest. Thus, they began to follow her to the hole she chose. Then, sitting in the darkness waiting for the enemy to finish unleashing death, the men talked to the dog. They assured her that everything was going to be all right. Wynne noted those voicing these positive thoughts appeared to help his combat buddies believe the bombs were not going to touch them either.

The hours in the shelters emphasized what all those serving in World War II often tried to ignore—death was always a heartbeat away. In most cases there was no warning of when they might draw their last breath. You could dodge a thousand bullets and then step on a land mine. You could survive a dozen battles and be brought down by a local disease. Death was simply everywhere. And dying so far from home shook many to the core. Therefore a chance to read a letter from a loved one, watch a movie about life in the States, or look through a magazine allowed these young men to momentarily escape the stark and haunting realities of their fragile lives.

In the summer of 1944, Wynne picked up a magazine and

settled into his bunk. He wanted to read some good news and forget the bad news he saw every day. As he thumbed through *Yank Magazine* he noted an advertisement begging G.I.s to mail in photos of their company mascots. The magazine's editors would review all the entries and pick one as representative of every mascot in the war. Encouraged by his fighting brothers in the 5th Air Force, 26th Photo Recon Squadron, Wynne grabbed his camera, placed the Yorkie in his helmet, and, with a host of friends waving at the pooch, took a picture. That image would not only win the contest, making Smoky the "Champion Mascot of the Pacific Theater," but it would be printed in magazines and newspapers all across the United States with a caption describing the miniscule mutt as a Yorkie Doodle Dandy. The dog that had been tossed away in the jungle was now a symbol of American military pride.

This award not only brought fame but also new responsibilities. Overnight Smoky became a morale officer. Men stationed in the region would visit the camp just to meet the dog and watch her perform. What was quickly apparent was that Smoky loved the applause and attention. Even when Wynne was doing his regular Army job, she worked the crowd in the photo tent with a series of stunts. Through a bit of misfortune, her command performances would soon find an even larger audience.

Wynne came down with what the locals called jungle fever. When his temperature rose to 105, he was taken off the front lines and sent to a hospital in Australia. The sick soldier took the pooch with him and even convinced the doctors to allow Smoky to stay in his hospital ward. The dog quickly became a favorite with the patients and, when Wynne was able to get out of bed, army nurses convinced him to allow Smoky to entertain wounded servicemen in the hospital's other wings. Wynne now sensed his dog's contributions to the war effort could be much greater than his own and spent extra time dreaming up new tricks. He was just putting them into action and dreaming of Smoky becoming the canine version of Bob Hope when he was called back to active duty.

As the Americans pushed the Japanese west, the Army needed Wynne's skills as a photographer to capture their movements. It was time for the soldier to get back to the front lines, pick up his camera, jump in a plane, and go back to work. Ironically, to get back in the air Wynne had to hop aboard a ship. It was on an LST transport headed toward the Philippines that the Yorkie moved beyond performing mascot and into the realm of an almost psychic hero.

If the Japanese had any hope of turning the war around in their favor, they had to prevent American troop ships from reaching battle zones. Thus, every transport and liberty vessel wore a huge target. An enemy scout plane spotted the convoy early in the morning. By midday the Japanese navy launched a full-force attack. From the air and sea the enemy tossed everything they had at the Americans, including kamikaze planes.

As a photographer who had recorded so much of the war from the air, Wynne was fascinated and horrified by this close-up view of the action. All around him men were frantically trying to ward off wave after wave of Japanese planes while also watching helplessly as huge shells flew through the air toward their vessel. The noise of combat was deafening. Ducking low to stay out of the line of fire, occasionally reaching down to pet the tiny companion hovering by his side, Wynne observed men dying all around him. This astonishing scene made the small air raids that he had experienced in New Guinea look like a child's game.

If the Yorkie realized how fragile life was at this moment, she didn't show it. With chaos encircling her, Smoky calmly watched, her little brown eyes following the movement of men racing across the ship's deck and watching an explosion churn up the ocean. When a huge shell hit and rocked the ship, many men screamed, but the dog only glanced in the direction of impact and didn't even yelp. Wynne marveled at the canine's almost placid demeanor. She hadn't been prepared or trained for these horrifying conditions, but she handled them like a seasoned combat veteran. If only he could have her strength and her faith.

As Wynne huddled and waited to see who would claim victory in this sea battle, he was joined by eight other soldiers. Like him, they were fish out of water. With no assigned duties they helplessly watched others take on the enemy. For what seemed like an eternity, the nine G.I.s crouched and pointed out elements of the battle. They cursed their inability to contribute and at the same time they prayed for all the madness to end. They were angry, wanting to help, and they sensed a need to be a part of saving lives, but no one was calling on them to do anything more than be spectators. It was an impotent role that made them feel like children.

As his comrades continued to observe the horrific scene playing out before them, Wynne looked back toward his dog. Smoky was suddenly excited and doing everything she could to get her master's attention. Wynne was confused. Nothing had changed. They were still tucked safely behind a big truck out of the line of fire. So what had the Yorkie seen that had so upset her?

Wynne reached to comfort Smoky, but she would have none of it. Instead, she moved away from him. Afraid the dog might roam into danger, the army photographer slowly crept after the tiny mutt. Finally, she stopped and turned, her concerned eyes seemingly begging the man to hurry up. Working his way to her side, he fell on his belly and pulled her to his chest. Once she was secure, Wynne looked back toward his comrades. He was about to wave when an artillery shell exploded spreading shrapnel in the same area he had just vacated. In an instant, every one of his friends had died.

How had Smoky known what was coming? Had she heard it or sensed it? Was it a skill she had developed while in the air raid bunkers? Or had God placed that dog in the foxhole just so Wynne would survive this battle? A few days later, when they were setting up camp in Luzon and getting ready to help retake the central Philippines, Wynne found himself still wondering how Smoky knew the shell was about to hit.

Over the next few months, Wynne was assigned to a number of vital photo reconnaissance missions. A dozen of those trips placed him over heavy combat areas. On each of these assignments he took his four-pound good luck charm along. As he shot photos of Japanese bases, naval convoys, and airfields, he kept an eye on the small dog. Never once, even when flack was filling the skies around them, did she ever get agitated. It was as if she was sure they were somehow protected from being knocked out of the air. How did she know that? Had she been given some kind of sixth sense or an ability to see an angel of death no man could envision? He had no clue, but he now had great faith in her instincts. If Smoky felt safe, so did he.

In February 1945, even with the Americans now seizing the clear advantage, casualties remained heavy. Though retreating, the Japanese were not giving up. The enemy still believed if they could knock out enough American ships and planes, the tide of the war would turn in their favor. During this period Wynne was with a group from the Army Air Corps as they took control of what had been a Japanese airfield eighty miles north of Manila outside the small town of Lingayen. One specific problem arose as the construction crew made the strip ready for American military use. There was no way to securely string telephone wire from across the field and to the headquarters.

Telephone lines were essential to base operations. The calls from the front lines would sound an early alert thus allowing planes to get airborne before the Japanese fighters and bombers arrived. If they didn't get airborne, then the planes not only couldn't fight off the enemy but also they would be easy targets sitting on the ground.

Engineers explained the only way communication could be assured during attacks was to string the wires in small drainage pipes that ran beneath the dirt runways. Because the pipes were only eight inches across there was no way a man could crawl through them. As dirt and debris was piled up as high as four inches in places, pushing a line through the pipes would be impossible. And if they strung the lines above ground on poles, enemy planes could easily take them out on their first strike run.

The sad reality was that it would take three days of working round the clock for the crew to dig up drainage pipes, run wires through them and then reverse the process to make the runway usable. During that period the unit's forty planes would be grounded. If the Japanese raided there would be no air support, and it was likely the American aircraft would be destroyed where they sat. Also, with the planes on the ground, there could be no support flights or recon missions. That meant it was likely that many soldiers, sailors, and marines would die because of the lack of air support. But what other choice was there? The phone lines had to be strung.

As the top brass considered the issue, Sergeant Bob Gapp made a trip to Bob Wynne's tent. As the two talked, Gapp kept looking at Smoky. The dog, sensing she had a chance to grab some attention, began to perform a few of her tricks.

"She's smart," Gapp noted. Then, a few moments later he finally worked up the courage to ask the question that had driven him to seeking out Wynne. "Do you think Smoky could run through those pipes and take a phone wire from one side to the other?"

A few minutes later the two men and the dog were out on the runway. Dropping to his stomach, Wynne looked through one of the small culverts. While Smoky was only seven inches tall, even without the debris it would be a tight fit. And, because of the heavily corroded pipe's unstable and fragile state, just having the dog struggle to push through them might cause them to collapse. If that happened she would likely suffocate before anyone could dig down to her.

Wynne looked down at the trusting Yorkie. Men's lives depended on this base remaining open. The sooner the phone lines were strung the less the chance was of Americans having to make the ultimate sacrifice. Though everything in him demanded that he say no, Wynne looked back toward Gapp and nodded.

But before he readied his dog for the dangerous mission, he asked the sergeant for one promise. If the tunnel collapsed there had to be a crew ready to dig down to the spot and free the dog. After securing the other soldier's word, Wynne went to work setting up a plan for pint-size Smoky to accomplish this unique mission.

The phone lines were lightweight and on spools. Even a four-pound Yorkie would have no problem pulling one the sixty-foot length of the pipe. The problem was the dirt that was in the culverts. Would Smoky dig through the rubble or would she turn around and head back to the entrance? The success of the mission depended upon her determination to push forward. Thus, he had to be on the other end of the pipe urging her to come to him. For this to work, Smoky would have to completely surrender her trust to Wynne.

After a crew was assembled to dig the dog out if the pipe collapsed, Wynne attached the phone line to Smoky's collar and handed the dog to Gapp. The sergeant held the pooch in his arms until Wynne made his way to the other side. Gapp then pushed Smoky into the tiny opening. On the other end, Wynne began to call her name.

Initially the dog was hesitant. Finally, after a few moments of listening to her master's pleas echoing through the metal tube, she began the trek. As Wynne could not see her, Gapp yelled out from time to time to mark the dog's progress. Ten feet became twenty; after digging away a mound of dirt, the Yorkie managed another ten feet. She was almost halfway when Gapp called out she was caught. With Wynne urging her on, the dog, now working in almost complete darkness, began to dig. It took several seconds for her tiny paws to push enough dirt to the side to squeeze through a fist-sized opening and continue her trek. Once beyond that obstacle, she picked up speed and was at a full gallop when she all but leaped into Wynne's arms on the far side. With scores of men cheering, he reached down and removed the phone line. She had made it. By late in the afternoon all the lines had been strung and the little dog had become an honorary member of the communications crew. That night even hardened officers discussed whether the miniature pooch shouldn't get a special citation. Rather than a medal, she was awarded a steak.

Though she remained in the combat zones for the remainder of the summer, the Yorkie was never again called upon to do another military job. As Americans rushed toward Japan and President Truman ordered two atomic bombs to be dropped, Smoky resumed her duties as Wynne's companion and her company's mascot.

When the war ended, Army regulations prevented the much-heralded dog from going home with her master. Wynne tried to fight the red tape but appeared to finally give in to the military's orders to find the little hero a local home. However, he secretly placed Smoky inside an oxygen mask and smuggled the Yorkie back to Cleveland, Ohio. The army would not find out about Wynne's disobeying military regulations until he was a civilian. But word did get out. On December 7, 1945, exactly four years after World War II began, *The Cleveland Press* ran a front-page story on the courageous canine. The feature included a photo of Smoky wearing a small army uniform.

Bob Wynne used the publicity the story generated to launch a new career. Perfecting a stage show, he and Smoky performed at fairs, theaters, orphanages, schools, and hospitals all over the nation. The pair also entertained thousands in V.A. facilities. They even headlined one of the first live television series in Ohio. Before her death on February 21, 1957, the war hero would perform before more than a million people.

On Veteran's Day in 2005, a two-ton bronze and granite statue was placed on the four-pound dog's grave. It read, "Smoky, Yorkie Doodle Dandy, and Dogs of All Wars." But this incredible tribute was not the last chapter in Smoky's matchless story.

In July 2012, an Australian paper finally solved the mystery of how Smoky got into that jungle foxhole. While stationed in Australia, an American Army nurse, Lt. Grace Heidenreich, had purchased the Yorkie from a Melbourne pet store. When Heidenreich was transferred to New Guinea she took the dog with her. When she was on duty, the Yorkie ran away from the hospital and the nurse assumed it had died. Little did she realize her lost dog would live through her jungle trek and emerge as the smallest hero of World War II. In a final ironic twist, Bob Wynne discovered that Heidenreich was not only still alive, but she lived just three blocks from his house. It was almost as if Smoky had somehow brought the two together as the final proof of her incredible magical life.

8

LOVE

WHAT THE WORLD NEEDS NOW
AND ALWAYS

A flower cannot blossom without sunshine,
and man cannot live without love.
—Max Müller

Therapy dogs are unique. At first glance their job does not seem in any way heroic. They don't dive into rivers to save drowning people, they don't run into burning barns and lead animals out through the smoke and flames, and they don't alert soldiers to bombs or enemy troop movements. They are quiet, reserved, and patient. But for three generations these four-footed therapists have offered love and healing in ways that even trained clergymen or experienced counselors have never been able to master. And, when on the job, these canines are tireless workers who absorb the fears, emotions, and hopelessness that have been consuming the human spirit, and somehow exchange them for rays of warm sunshine. On the surface this would seem to be impossible, but it happens thousands of times a day all over the world. And countless lives might well have been saved or, at the very least, dramatically altered, because of the works of these special dogs.

The history of therapy dogs is usually traced to a World War II veteran named Smoky. As you likely remember from the previous chapter, Smoky was a starving, lost Yorkshire terrier found in the jungles of New Guinea. While she would earn the title of a certified hero on the battlefield, Smoky spent part of the war and more than a decade after visiting patients in hospitals. For badly wounded G.I.s her presence brought relief from suffering as well as moments of sheer joy and happiness. In some cases she was with men, offering comfort and compassion, as they drew their final breaths. The last touch these brave fighting soldiers felt on earth was that of a four-pound dog that presented them with completely unconditional love. That was the beginning of the therapy dog movement, and from that one diminutive hero it has grown to include tens of thousands of dogs of all sizes and breeds.

Jill Cucaz was a Virginia fifth-grade teacher and the proud owner of a golden retriever when she discovered the incredible potential of therapy dogs. Through reading programs at her school as well as during hospital and nursing home visits, she watched countless dogs bring smiles and motivation to scores of people. She soon grew to think of them as heart healers. The New Jersey born Jill was thus inspired to have more than just a pet; her Dakotah was going to be trained for a job. He was going to have a purpose. Little did the elementary school teacher know at that time that this simple decision would take her into places filled with broken hearts and unmeasured fears and that her dog would become an inspiration during the moments when modern America was shaken to its core.

Jill teamed up with Hope Animal-Assisted Crisis Response, trained her dog for months while he earned his certification, and then began to take her Dakotah to hospitals. As she and her retriever walked through cancer wards, she watched faces light up time and time again. It was as if he was the energy these kids needed to shine. One night in Virginia Commonwealth University Medical Center, she strolled by the room of a teenage girl battling cancer. The young woman was sullen and quiet. Her mother, who sat by her bed, was crying. Chemo had taken its toll and the frail teen sat in bed, her eyes staring blankly at a television. Just as devastating was the mother seeing her daughter's body and spirit waste. Cancer had zapped both women of all hope.

After carefully sizing up the situation, Jill quietly asked if the girl would like to visit with her dog. The immediate response was no, but just before the teacher and Dakotah moved on, the mother called out. Her voice shaking, she begged Jill to come and visit. Even if her daughter was too tired to spend a few moments with the retriever, the insecure mother wanted to meet the calm, happy animal.

As if he understood what the woman needed, Dakotah walked over to the mother, laid his big head in her lap, and the petting began. Over the next five minutes her tears were replaced by a huge smile. Soon the petting gave way to hugging and laughter. For a few minutes the agony that had all but squeezed the life from her heart disappeared, replaced by a newfound hope.

As the teen observed her mother and the dog play, her face remained hard, her look vacant. It still appeared she wanted no part of the action. The mother, praying the dog could give her daughter some sense of peace, asked Jill a simple question, "Could you put him on my daughter's bed so she can really see him?"

The schoolteacher got a towel, placed it beside the frail girl, and lifted Dakotah up onto the bed. The trained dog remained still, his large brown eyes locked onto the patient until her hand tentatively eased down between his ears. He then nosed forward and licked her cheek. Surprised, the girl's brown eyes grew as large as saucers, and, after lifting her bald head from the pillow, she studied the dog, smiled, and then giggled. In an instant a bit of color rushed to her deathly pale face. When Dakotah kissed her again her giggles grew into laughter. Suddenly the almost emaciated patient had energy and life. With no hesitation she wrapped her arms around the dog and hugged him. It was an embrace that would go on for minutes. And, in that instant, the cancer that had taken such a huge toll on her body and spirit had been beaten back. For the moment it seemed as though the disease was in full retreat.

Jill looked from the bed to back where the mother sat. The woman had tears rushing from her eyes and down her face. As the daughter continued to pet and enjoy Dakotah, the mother called Jill over and whispered, "She hasn't laughed in weeks. I had even given up on ever seeing her smile again. None of us could bring her any hope and nothing could reduce her pain. I think she had given up. But look at her now!"

On a regular basis Jill and Dakotah continued to visit that room on the cancer ward. They watched the girl's struggle to live turn into a march toward health. In time the once frail child left the hospital with a newfound strength and determination, and her dramatic change in attitude all started with a visit from a dog.

Over the next two years Jill watched this story play out time and again. Kids with no hope suddenly came to life when Dakotah entered a room. Parents who had given up believed again. Her dog was a prescription that often proved stronger than the latest miracle drug or surgical technique. When hope was gone, the dog stepped in and dragged it back into the room.

For years Jill and Dakotah, as well as another golden she had trained for therapy, Custer, made their weekly rounds at VCU and other requested locations. All the time they worked their magic they never really imagined ever reaching beyond the region where they lived. But then, on September 11, 2001 everything changed.

On that morning when the world came to a stop, Jill was teaching her elementary school class. For those within easy driving distance of New York City and Washington, D.C., the news shook them to the core. Jill, like almost everyone in the area, knew people who worked in the areas struck by airplanes the terrorists had hijacked and used for bombs. Her first thought naturally centered on whether someone she had known had died that day.

Yet she could not allow her own shock and fears to show. She had young students who were also facing this news with a lack of understanding. This overwhelming moment had immediately stolen a bit of their childhood innocence. All around them adults were obviously frightened and insecure. While a few moments before everything was solid and normal, now there was an atmosphere of fear and apprehension. What would happen next? How Jill wished she had brought Dakotah to work that day. While she didn't know how to fully address this situation, he would have found a way to somehow make the world seem a bit safer.

A few days later, as Americans watched the news media's coverage of the disaster, Jill's phone rang. Hope Animal-Assisted Crisis Response had been asked to go to New York City. The dogs were needed as a coping mechanism for people who had lost everything. So in the weeks after the disaster, while almost everyone else was fleeing the place where terrorists had brought the country to a standstill, Jill, Dakotah, and Custer were going there on a mission.

The Family Assistance Center on Pier 94 was located at West 53rd and West 54th Street in New York City. It had been set as a gathering point for those whom 9/11 had left jobless or homeless. From the day it opened, city, state, and federal agencies set up offices there to distribute aid and provide information on what was going on with the recovery of bodies from what was left of the World Trade Center. The facility offered meals, childcare, and free access to telephones and computers. On a daily basis the center also helped thousands whose financial world had been ripped apart when the terrorists attacked. But it was far more than just a resource for those who needed physical aid. It quickly became apparent that Pier 94's highest calling was to help those who had lost loved ones in the attack. This was a place where suffering hearts gathered to try to make sense of what made no sense. And day after day they came back to sit and wait and hope.

Few realize the incredible fallout created by 9/11. Even today the number of people whose lives were forever changed when the World Trade Center towers collapsed remains so staggering as to be incomprehensible. But the numbers do tell a story. In its first two months of operation, 229,000 people walked into the Family Assistance Center. That was almost 4,000 a day.

As you can imagine, even in a city the size of New York, clergy could not handle all the needs for counseling. So many people just sat, looked at the photos of the lost that had been pasted on the walls, and mourned at the makeshift memorials that had been positioned under those pictures. Many times men, women, and children, grandparents and parents, husbands and wives, and friends and partners just sat mutely on the pews that lined the blue carpeted room and stared hopelessly into space. And, even over the noise created by numerous agencies doing their jobs, the sound of sobs could still be heard.

Jill had no idea what to expect as she and her husband walked their dogs into the facility for the first time. Wearing her green Hope Animal-Assisted Crisis Response shirt, the schoolteacher stopped just inside the main entrance and studied a building that seemed to go on forever. Thousands of people were either milling around or sitting in the pews. Hundreds of teddy bears had been brought in to comfort the children who had lost loved ones. Men and women from every branch of the military were there involved in various duties. The Red Cross and a number of other nonprofit organizations had booths set up and were offering food, clothing, and spiritual guidance. As Jill's eyes darted from one place to another, it was almost overwhelming. So many people were trying so hard to help and yet there just didn't seem to be any answers.

Though that day had a raw feel to it, the building was warm. Yet the comfortable temperature could not begin to make up for the incredible sense of loss that was everywhere. The sadness and despair were so overwhelming that she could both see and feel it. It was like a heavy weight pushing down on her shoulders and demanding to be allowed into her heart. She glanced down at Dakotah and noted that he seemed to feel it as well. His face was solemn, his manner reserved, and his always wagging tail still.

As her husband took Custer in one direction, Jill guided Dakotah past long rows of despondent people. They were sitting almost shoulder to shoulder on long benches. Some were likely waiting to take a promised ferry ride down to view the place where their loved ones had died and were still buried in the rubble that had once been two skyscrapers. Others were seeking food or emergency funds. Some seemed to have no real objective or goals. They just looked lost as if they had wandered in and couldn't bear to leave.

In the other places she had visited, people had always immediately responded to her dog. Their faces lit up and hands reached forward the instant the animal walked into the room. But today it was different. Some noticed, a few called out, but most just continued to mournfully stare straight ahead. It was as if Jill, Dakotah, and the whole world were invisible.

Looking down the long row of benches, studying face after face, Jill's eyes landed on two small girls, likely early elementary school age. They were cute, well-dressed children who, though reserved, were obviously completely aware of their surroundings. Their eyes were clear and, when they saw Dakotah, their faces broke out in huge smiles. Though they were still more than a hundred feet away, Jill sensed a connection that was so strong she went against one of the principle rules of therapy work. She dropped the leash, leaving Dakotah on his own.

The golden retriever did not hesitate. In a room filled with thousands of people, some now calling out to him, his focus was only on those two little girls. Picking up the pace until he reached a steady trot, he moved forward with Jill behind him jogging to keep up. Nothing would deter him and the big dog did not stop until he was face to face with the two children.

Without hesitation they both tossed their arms around the

retriever. He patiently stood, his mug of a face framed in a grin, as they pulled on his fur and smothered him with kisses. With Jill watching, the girls laughed and giggled and cooed. Finally, after almost five minutes of nonstop loving, one of them looked up at the schoolteacher and explained why this unexpected visit meant so much to her.

In a hushed tone she began, "Our mommy didn't come home from work in the Trade Center. She is still there. She's never coming home. Mommy was going to get her own golden retriever puppy for us to raise. She couldn't wait. He was going to be her dog that she shared with us. But she died two weeks before it was to be delivered."

Jill's eyes grew misty as she listened to the story. She didn't know what to say. She was fumbling for words when the child picked up the conversation.

"What's your dog's name?"

"Dakotah."

The little girl smiled, "Mommy so loved golden retrievers and she must have sent Dakotah to tell us wherever she is that she is all right. He brought her love to us. I can feel it. Can't you?"

While the children continued to play with her dog, Jill turned away and through tear-filled eyes once more looked at the mass of humanity surrounding her. All of them were looking for reasons to hope. They all needed to have someone bring them a sign that things would get better and the pain would someday go away. And at least for these two children, her dog had done that. For the moment, he was a light in a place filled with absolute darkness.

Over the next few hours Dakotah and Custer were embraced

by hundreds of people. Unlike the little girls, many could not smile as they held the dogs; they could only cry. For them it seemed as though the dogs had become a substitute for the loved ones they would never again see. Being with animals that never said a word but just offered unconditional love provided an opportunity for these survivors to at least imagine they were once more hugging the ones they had lost on September 11.

As it grew time to leave and Jill worked through the crowd toward the door, she noted that her husband was standing to one side smiling. Moving to the spot, she was amazed to see Custer wrestling with someone wearing a uniform. As she looked more closely she realized the man was a four-star army general and was laughing so hard his cheeks had turned red. Finally getting to his feet, the officer petted the dog and said, "That is the best five minutes I have had in days. Thank God for your dogs." It was the perfect way for that first visit to end.

Jill made several trips to Pier 94 and the response was always the same. The dogs seemed to work miracle after miracle. It was only when she returned home from those trips that she realized the heavy emotional toll that had been placed on the animals. After spending so much time with the hurting souls in the center, both Dakotah and Custer did little but sleep for days. Bringing a bit of light to a dark world had extracted a steep price. It was as if it had taken all their energy just to carry the burdens those victims had shared with them. Yet the next time she put on the green shirt and was ready to go back to do more therapy work, they bounced up and rushed to her side. For them this was not just another outing; it had become the focal point of their lives. They literally lived for it.

The next decade would see Dakotah and Custer, and later Willoughby, work with victims of tornados, floods, and fires. They went to Montana, New Orleans, and Florida. They witnessed the damage done by Hurricane Katrina and Superstorm Sandy. Over the course of those visits thousands found hope by just touching the dogs. Jill lost count of the tears and the smiles she saw but she never forgot the way her animals somehow offered some healing hope to people who had lost everything. And during these visits to the huddled masses, in spite of the vast numbers of refugees, the dogs touched hearts one life at a time.

For Jill the power of a dog's ability to heal the spirit and erase fears was fully realized when she made another visit to VCU. As soon as she walked onto the children's wing a nurse rushed up to her and informed her that under no circumstances was she to go in a certain room. There was a young boy in that room who was recovering from cosmetic surgery to repair facial injuries suffered when a neighbor's dog had gotten out of its pen and bitten the child's face. If a family member had not witnessed the attack and wrestled the dog away, the seven-year-old would have likely died. While his physical injuries were severe, they were healing, but his emotional scars were so deep that dogs visited him in his nightmares and he could not even watch a dog on a TV screen.

Jill noted the room and hurried Willoughby past the open door and down the hall to visit with other children. These room-to-room visits went on for most of the afternoon. Finally it was time to go and she made one final stop in the hall to allow a small girl to pet her big golden retriever. It was then she noticed the bite victim poke his head around the corner of his room's door and take a quick peek at the activity in the hall. Over the course of the next two minutes the child would pop his head in and then out several more times. Finally, he slowly snuck completely out of his room and touched Willoughby's tail. He then raced back in to hide. The next time he appeared he patted the dog's back. This little game continued for several minutes until he finally crept cautiously up to the big dog's head, looked into his soft brown eyes and stroked his big head. Willoughby sighed, laid down, and the boy sat down beside him.

As the news of this incredible event made its way up and down the hospital's various wings, nurses and doctors raced to the location to witness the timid child now playing with the almost one-hundred-pound dog. They couldn't believe it. With no encouragement, the scene played out for half an hour until the boy lay down against the dog's side and fell asleep. As he did, more than a dozen staff members cried.

Jill and her dogs represent tens of thousands of therapy teams that give their time to share love with those whom some refer to as the least of these. The small miracles created by these animals' visits show the incredible true and genuine power of unconditional canine love.

Several years ago, I had a sable-and-white collie that I used in therapy work. Every week my dog and I would go to nursing homes. On one of those visits I was ushered into a dark room where a thin, drawn woman sat in a wheelchair. As she looked up I noted her eyes were hollow and lifeless. I smiled but her expression didn't change. When I said, "Hello," she remained mute.

After being nudged by a nurse, I signaled for Lady to go across the room to the woman. As trained, the collie sat beside the wheelchair and laid her head in the resident's lap. After a few seconds the woman lifted her hand and slowly began to stroke my dog's broad head. This continued for a few moments and then the elderly patient looked up at me. She studied me for a moment before posing an observation, "Your dog looks like Lassie."

I just nodded. I had grown used to the fact that to most people almost all sable and white collies looked like Lassie. As I watched her pet Lady, the woman got a faraway look in her eyes and began to talk.

"I was just a young mother when I took my children to see the movie *Lassie Come Home.* They so loved that film. In fact, over the next few years I took them to all six of the Lassie movies. And years later my grandkids used to always come over on Sunday nights and watch *Lassie* on TV with me. I can still remember an episode where June Lockhart got her foot caught in a bear trap and Lassie had to rescue her before a cougar attacked. That one scared the grandkids to death. Oh, those were special times."

Over the course of the next ten minutes the elderly woman grew more and more animated as she shared memories of watching Lassie with her kids and grandkids. She laughed, cried a little and continued to pet my dog as she excitedly jumped from one story to the next. Finally, she stopped speaking, quit petting Lady's head, and the life drained from her eyes. It was then the nurse signaled it was time to go, and my therapy collie and I stepped out into the hallway.

Once we moved into a well-lit area I noted the nurse was crying. I quickly asked if I had done anything wrong. The woman shook her head and said, "No, Mrs. Burton has Alzheimer's and has not spoken in four years."

The woman never said another word. None of our future

visits were able to open that long locked door to her mind. But for a brief while on one rainy Wednesday, a collie gave a few memories back to a lost woman. That is the power of a therapy dog.

Jill Cucaz noted early on that her therapy dogs did not have to amaze to make a difference. They didn't have to perform stunts or learn elaborate tricks. All they really had to do was love unconditionally. Most often in life, when we are overwhelmed by a big thing it is the little things that make a difference. The little things are what bring the first steps to healing. Perhaps the most unsung of all the canine heroes are those dogs that come in all shapes and sizes and embrace the jobs of reaching the world's least of these with little more than love, a wet kiss, and a wagging tail. These are such little things but they are oh so very powerful!

9

COURAGE

★ ★ ★

THE POWER OF DIRECTED PASSION

Courage is not the absence of fear, but rather the judgment
that something else is more important than fear.
—James Neil Hollingworth

For Kendal Plank, April 20, 1996, started just like any other Saturday. She was alone in her home in Tucson, Arizona, while her husband, Jerry, worked a weekend shift in the mines. Yet as Kendal went about her household chores, she didn't lack for company. Brandy, her seven-month-old, fifteen-pound, tan cocker spaniel puppy, was eagerly bouncing around the room. As if celebrating that she had her mistress all to herself, the energetic tangle of curly hair and oversized feet was shadowing the woman's every move. Brandy was not just underfoot on this Saturday morning, she was also over foot and beside foot too.

Kendal had recently celebrated her forty-fourth birthday and there were times when she wondered if she wasn't just a bit too old to keep up with the brown-eyed tousle of fur that seemed to be constantly getting in her way. Brandy was anything but laid back. She rarely wanted to rest and constantly demanded attention. In fact, there were moments when it seemed the lovable puppy was really trouble on the run. If Brandy wasn't chasing Kendal, she was tearing up a shoe or knocking over a lamp. She jumped in the middle of unmade beds, knocked over trash, dragged dirty clothes out of the hamper, and used magazines as chew toys. It seemed obvious to Kendal that the person who called the dog man's best friend never had to house train a cocker spaniel. It was a task that at times proved impossible and always tried the woman's patience. Yet just when she was about to scold the little bundle of hyper-energy, Brandy would turn those innocent eyes her way, grab a ball, or push her head into a paper sack and become the class clown. Her antics more than made up for the moments when Brandy all but destroyed the peaceful solitude that the modest home offered Kendal and her husband. After all, this unique combination of aggravation and devotion are what had long made the spaniel one of the world's favorite breeds.

Cocker spaniels trace their roots back more than six centuries to Spain. Brought to England before Europeans even discovered America, they were used to track, flush, and retrieve woodcocks. That required an energy level that boarded on hyperactivity. They literally had to run through the woods and fields for hours at a time, never stopping for rest. Once on the trail they were relentless, continuing to push forward in their quest long after their human companions had completely played out. While that was great on the hunt, it could make for a stressful relationship at home. With its high energy and endless curiosity, a spaniel, not challenged and left to his or her own devices, was capable of getting into a lot of trouble. Even carefully monitored, the breed often tested those humans who dared bring them into their world.

On this Saturday morning, Kendal's morning chores took twice as long because Brandy not only supervised the woman's every move, but also got involved in trying to help. Between grabbing at dusting cloths and playing chase with a broom, the puppy had become part of the problem. Then there was the hair she left everywhere and the constant yipping. Even though Kendal loved her dog, she wondered at times, especially when being literally hounded as she worked, if having a pet was not more trouble than it was worth.

As Kendal sat down for lunch, Brandy, who had been racing through the house since dawn, finally seemed to tire. Heading to her favorite spot next to an overstuffed chair, the puppy lay down, moaned a few times, then finding a position that was comfortable, fell into a deep sleep. For Kendal, who had combined as much play and work as possible, Brandy's steady breathing and closed eyes were an answered prayer.

As she nibbled on leftovers, Kendal laughed at her own judgment in adopting Brandy. The dog was anything but a stress reliever. If anything she was a chaos creator, and the woman sensed she would always be that way. Kendal was a social worker who scheduled court hearings and was responsible for appointing attorneys in child custody cases as well as dealing with fighting parents and often emotionally abused children; it would have seemed an elderly cat would have been a far better prescription for the woman's emotional needs. Yet in Brandy Kendal saw a selfless love and forgiving spirit that she rarely witnessed with those she dealt with at work. During days filled with mind-numbing tirades and threats, the spaniel offered the kind of devotion and acceptance that Kendal needed. So even as much trouble as the pup usually was, it was trouble that could be easily fixed and handled. And, unlike many areas of her job, there were reasons and remedies in dealing with the puppy. Logic could even be applied to most situations and therefore this tornado of canine energy was a blessing. In fact, Kendal told her friends that, in an often hopeless and cruel world, Brandy was the rock that God had placed in her life to remind her that he was with her.

Glancing up from the table and through a window, Kendal stared out at a beautiful spring day. Though many felt the lack of trees and grass made the desert a wasteland, during this time of the year it had a stark, rare beauty that demanded attention. With the temperatures moderate and the arid plants thriving, she should have been out enjoying the area's natural beauty that was only a stone's throw from her front door. What a shame she couldn't put Brandy on a leash and take it all in. Besides the fact that household duties were demanding her attention, the woman was also well aware of the gang activity that had invaded her neighborhood. This once peaceful part of Tucson now had been enveloped in an undercurrent of violence that was motivated by misguided and bored youth looking for ways to fill their time. On several occasions Kendal had seen fights and brawls firsthand. While driving down the neighborhood streets she had watched drug deals go down and knew of innocent children sucked into the gang lifestyle by promises of an exciting life and easy money. At night her sleep was sometimes disturbed by gunfire and the pounding, wall-shaking rhythms that echoed from car stereos. In this world kids seemed to race toward death with wild abandon, and the police could do nothing about it. Because of this culture, there was a fear that hovered over the area like a dense fog. Even in the daytime, men, women, and children looked over their shoulders whenever they heard a noise and always kept their door locked and bolted.

As Kendal contemplated the loss of innocence in her own world, Brandy peacefully slept, oblivious to the danger that lurked just outside her door. If only Kendal could somehow find that sense of security. If only she could forget the troubles that had invaded her neighborhood and the problems she dealt with at work. Yet, as long as she lived in this area, that would be impossible. The dangers, though often unseen, were always there. And, as Kendal's once placid and family-oriented neighborhood was now a war zone, even she and her husband had adopted a new way of life. They had ceased sitting out in their yard on cool evenings. And though she had hated to give in to the evil forces in her world, they had even installed iron bars over their windows. So while the couple couldn't hold back the gang wars that surrounded them on every corner, with the security of the bars, they believed they could now keep the violence of the outside world from spilling into their quiet home. But in a very real sense, the bars also made them prisoners in their own house.

Glancing back at her small puppy, Kendal wondered if the spaniel had been the right choice. Many of her friends had suggested a German shepherd or Doberman. Those breeds could not just scare away intruders, but would also lay down their lives for their owners. Much more than the bars on the windows, a big, powerful dog was what every home in this area needed. Yet, Kendal had passed on that solid advice, opting for a puppy that could not even intimidate the local alley cats. Had that been a mistake? It was a question she hoped she never had to answer.

A few blocks from where Kendal sat, Brett Christopher Garcia was restlessly pacing. The unemployed high school dropout was bored with life and deeply dissatisfied with his station in in the world. He thirsted for something better than the mind-numbing routine of watching television and partying with his friends. He also needed money to fuel addictions born from hopelessness and monotony. Garcia was a mirror image of the kids Kendal Plank saw in her work. He was angry and directionless. He had no respect for authority and felt little love in his life. Worse yet, his friends, those who mentored his every move, were older and had no regard for the fragility of life. They lived in the moment, stealing what they needed and using it to fuel a temporary high. Rather than embracing life, they were in a sense running from it.

As directionless as the Planks' puppy, Garcia was a lot more dangerous. The police already knew him well. A gang member with a multiple arrest record dating back to junior high, the cops had labeled the short, lean nineteen-year-old a time bomb waiting to explode. Even after several stays in jail and numerous trips to therapy, Garcia remained unpredictable, moody, and often violent. Day by day he grew more hardened and coarse, his potential and talents buried deeper and deeper by the pain and depravity he experienced on the streets.

Looking at the image of the young man mindlessly watching television, it would have been hard for anyone to believe that Garcia was once as carefree and happy as Brandy. There was a time when he had exhibited that same kind of zest for life and desire to please. Yet where the spaniel had been loved, the young man had been ignored, shoved aside, pushed away from the attention and encouragement he needed. By his teens the only people who seemed to want him were members of a south-side gang. Craving acceptance, the young man eagerly joined a group who thought of robbery as a way to get ahead and murder as a recreational sport. It was little wonder that Garcia quickly became as devoted to his gang family as Brandy was to the Planks. Immersed in this perverted world where right and wrong had been reversed, the

boy adopted attitudes that showed little regard for his own welfare and no respect for anyone else.

By the time Kendal placed her dishes in the sink, Garcia had
downed his lunch of a six-pack of beer. For dessert he smoked a
couple of joints. High, angry, and unfulfilled, fueled by a rage
he didn't comprehend, the teen then left his home to find the
money he needed to purchase more booze and drugs. When
he couldn't dig up any of his friends, the boy decided to enact a
more dangerous plan. Unsuccessful at begging for a handout, he
would take one. All he needed was a few items to pawn and those
could be found at homes throughout the neighborhood.

As he wandered down the streets, his dark eyes moving from
side to side in search of a target, the shabbily dressed Garcia was
a person to be avoided. Business owners watched him with both
apprehension and suspicion as he stared into their shops. Much
like the rattlesnakes that stalked the nearby desert, this was a man
to be feared. Those in his path crossed the streets in order to not
have to face his hollow and foreboding glare.

For almost an hour Garcia wandered from block to block.
The cars he came across were locked, the homes he studied were
obviously occupied, and no one had left anything of value sitting in their yards. Then, not long after he passed the corner of
West Ina and North Thornydale Roads, he spotted the Planks'
humble home. The heavy bars over all the windows and doors
should have immediately discouraged Garcia, but instead he was
intrigued. In his deluded state he figured if this home was that
heavily fortified, then there must be something of great value
behind those walls. Sulking into the shadows, the experienced
burglar scoped out all sides of the house. Coming closer he

listened for any signs of activity. With Brandy napping and Kendal quietly going about her housework, Garcia heard nothing. Grimly smiling, he figured he had discovered an easy answer to his financial problems. Now all he had to do was find a way inside. On the backside of the house the desperate young man spied what he had been looking for. There, almost out of sight, was a window that didn't have any protective bars. It was small, but not too small for the slightly built teen to squirm through.

Reaching into his pocket, Garcia pulled out a handgun. This was his security. The gun was the power he needed to confront any problem. It was his best friend. And, if he had to use it to deliver death to a stranger, so be it. He checked to make sure the weapon was fully loaded before shoving it into his waistband. Silently he approached the unsecured window, his dark eyes constantly shifting from side to side to make sure he wasn't being observed. With the agility of an acrobat, Garcia pulled up to the ledge and eased the unlocked window open. Silently, in an almost catlike fashion, he dropped to the floor. Listening before he moved, he was quickly satisfied that no one was home. So far this had been even easier than he had planned. Within a few moments he was sure he could grab something of value and steal back onto the streets. Buoyed by the security the gun gave him and empowered by mixture of alcohol and drugs in his system, he straightened up and noiselessly strolled into the main part of the home. As he silently moved forward he carefully surveyed each square foot of the house for items that could be easily turned into cash.

It was twenty minutes past 1:00 when Kendal heard a strange noise. At the same instant Brandy awoke. The dog rolled up on her side and quickly looked back toward the kitchen. The woman would have probably ignored the mysterious sound, passing it off as something outside, if the spaniel's hair hadn't bristled. A split second later, Brandy flew out of the room at breakneck speed on a mission that neither she nor Kendal fully understood.

Instinct, combined with her puppy's reaction, told Kendal that someone was in her home. She knew it was too early to be her husband; she assumed it had to be an intruder. Reaching for the phone, the now frightened woman quickly called her sister-in-law. After whispering her fears to the woman, Kendal quickly hung up and then dialed 9-1-1. When the dispatcher answered, Kendal explained that she thought there might be a stranger in the house.

As Kendal waited for instructions, the dog went into action. Rounding a corner the puppy came face to face with a man she had never seen. Spaniels are not usually an aggressive breed. In her time with the Planks, Brandy had proven herself to be more a high-energy teddy bear than a guard dog. Thus, her first impulse was to race up to a stranger and welcome him into her world. But this time it was different. For some reason she didn't respond in a friendly manner. Something caused her face to grow suddenly serious, her eyes intense, and her muzzle pulled back to reveal sharp white teeth. For the first time in her short life she was ready to fight something other than a passive dog toy.

Like a shepherd protecting her flock, the dog somehow knew what she had to do. And even if that meant sacrificing her life, she was ready. She observed Garcia for a few moments as if gauging his motives. Then, without even as much as a warning yelp the spaniel raced across the tile toward the man she sensed was a threat.

Garcia, his senses dulled by drugs and alcohol, panicked, and rather than kick the puppy to one side, the teen reached for his gun. As Brandy charged closer, Garcia pulled the pistol from his belt and squeezed off five shots. His aim was perfect. Two rounds hit the pup's back legs, the other three found their mark in the chest, stomach and jaw. Snarls and barks where suddenly replaced with cries and yelps as the dog fell to the floor.

When Kendal heard Brandy's moans, she dropped the phone. Without considering the consequences, like a mother intent on rescuing her child, the woman ran in the direction of the noise. As she dashed into the back room, Garcia turned his attention from the dog to the woman. Coldly he aimed the still smoking gun at Kendal. As their eyes met, she turned to run away, but before she could clear the door, he pulled the trigger twice more. Both bullets hit their mark and the woman fell to the floor, blood spurting from wounds to her liver and kidney. A now completely deranged Garcia knew he couldn't leave behind any witnesses. He thus had to snuff out the life of the woman who could identify him. His fear likely heighted by the sight of blood and his judgment severely impaired by alcohol and drugs, he was ready to close in for the kill. He figured one bullet delivered to the head from close range would likely be all that was needed. Then he could find some cash and goods and get out. This was not the clean operation he had planned, but he could still get what he wanted.

As Garcia moved slowly toward the woman struggling to crawl across the floor, he had no way of knowing that Kendal had already called 9-1-1. He didn't guess the Tucson police had several units on their way to the scene. He also couldn't have known that a police operator was still on the line and heard Kendal when she called out, "I've been shot!" As he dug into his pocket for bullets needed to reload his gun, Garcia didn't hear the dispatcher cry out to Kendal to stay calm. The only thing on his mind was finishing his job and shutting the woman up. Garcia would have done just that if something hadn't distracted him.

Left for dead in a pool of her own blood, Brandy slowly opened her eyes. Having been hit by five different rounds, she was suffering pain that she couldn't possibly comprehend. Yet as she stared across the floor to Kendal trying to crawl away from Garcia, an ancient echo from the past, bred into her kind for generations, roused her need to serve her master. In an act that was incomprehensible, Brandy pulled herself off the floor and moved between Kendal and the intruder. The puppy somehow found the strength to not only growl and bark, but to tear at Garcia's pants. Again and again he tired to shove her away, but she wouldn't let him. Snapping at his hands, feet, and anything else she could reach, the puppy seemed intent on giving her last ounce of strength for the woman who had been so devoted to the pup. Knocking Garcia from his feet, she didn't allow him to reload his gun. With a determination and loyalty that the gang member had never seen on the street, the dog fought on, delivering another painful bite for every blow she received.

Garcia was now bleeding from several bites. Unable to use the empty gun to shoot the dog, he tried to fight Brandy off with the gun's butt. Reacting quickly, the pup avoided direct hits as she continued to bite into the intruder's flesh. Though outweighing the dog by more than a hundred pounds, an exasperated Garcia must have felt completely overwhelmed. Forgetting about the woman on the floor and the things he'd hoped to steal and pawn, he raced to the back of the house and out the door. The injured dog followed every step of the way. And she didn't stop when they got outside.

Ignoring pain and blood loss, the severely wounded Brandy continued to bark and chase the offender down the street. Amazingly, the dog that should have been dead hounded Garcia's every step for over a block. The dog didn't quit terrorizing the man until he was well away from the house. Then, perhaps sensing things were under control, she raced back home and watched as paramedics stabilized her owner.

While Kendal was being transported to the hospital, Garcia tried to use alleys and back streets to evade capture. Yet his efforts to fight off the dog had cost him too much time. He had gotten only two blocks when he was surrounded by police officers. Why the young man didn't give up will never be known. Perhaps in his deluded state he couldn't fully understand his position or maybe his life was so without meaning and hope that he had a desire to die. With the police begging him to lay down his weapon and give up, in a final futile act the desperate teen raised his gun and coldly aimed it at the closest officer. A volley of shots rang out and Garcia fell to the ground mortally wounded. Yet even as police raced to the side of the misguided youth, the final battle in this war was far from over.

For three days Kendal Plank's doctors fought to save the woman. Bullets had heavily damaged her colon, liver, and one kidney and if paramedics had arrived just a few minutes later, Brandy's heroic actions would have been for naught and Kendal would have died at the scene on the floor where she fell when she was shot. Even with treatment at the scene and immediate emergency surgery at the hospital, the woman hovered close to death for days. Finally, on Tuesday, the social worker turned the corner.

In spite of massive blood loss and five different extensive wounds, Brandy somehow survived. Displaying the tenacity and fight she had used to save her mistress, the pup was well enough to go home on Monday. She was there, her stub of a tail happily wagging, and yelping loud enough to raise the roof when Kendal came home later in the week. Needless to say, it was an emotionally charged reunion.

Two months after the attack, both Brandy and Kendal attended a special ceremony given by the Tucson Police Department. At the event Brandy became the first nonhuman to receive the department's purple heart.

"I think that Brandy scared Garcia so badly that he had nothing left to do but flee," said Sgt. Michael Downing, head of the department's homicide unit. "The dog drove him away."

For Kendal Plank the horrific memories of that Saturday afternoon still haunt her. She doesn't believe she will ever get over the emotional impact of Brett Garcia's senseless acts of violence. Yet, for the rest of her life, Brandy offered the security Kendal needed to face each new day. Even when the pup tore up a sock or a shoe, Kendal didn't stay mad for too long. Who could? This pint-sized ball of fur had saved her owner's life with courage that knew no limits. Brandy may have been a puppy, but on a Saturday in April, she possessed an understanding that was rooted in a devotion that seemed divine in nature. Few men could have withstood the wounds she took and found the strength to continue to fight.

The question that would never be answered is what if Brandy

or a dog like her had come into Garcia's life when he was a child? Could the love and devotion of that dog have prevented the young man from taking the path he took? It is a thought worth pondering as cities across the country attempt to match dogs with abused children to find a way to soften hearts hardened by human abuse and rejection.

10

GRATITUDE

★ ★ ★

THE CHRISTMAS STABLE MIRACLE

Thankfulness is the beginning of gratitude.
Gratitude is the completion of thankfulness. Thankfulness may
consist merely of words. Gratitude is shown in acts.
—Henri Frédérich Amiel

Much more than humans, dogs are all about second and even third chances. They don't judge on appearances and are capable of forgiving almost any transgression. They believe in a person's potential even on their worst days. A dog loves unconditionally those who show it even a little bit of kindness. To our canine friends, what you did yesterday is not nearly as important as what you do today and what you can do tomorrow.

For humans and dogs life was tough in New York City in the early part of the 1900s. The region was overflowing with immigrants from Europe, jobs were scarce, housing was in short supply, and there were no social safety nets. If you were out of work or hungry, no one was going to buy you a meal. No person understood society's often cruel rules more than Thomas Gallagher.

In the fall of 1910, Gallagher had been walking the Brooklyn streets for days. During that time the ill-kempt, lanky young man had eaten what others had thrown out and slept on park benches. Though toughened by the hard life he had been dealt, the twenty-year-old was also scared. He was alone, wearing the only set of clothes he owned, and he had come to realize that no one cared if he lived or died. Like so many indigent young men who had filled the city looking for either handouts, work, or both, the citizens of New York didn't see him. It was as if he were invisible.

Earlier in the morning Gallagher killed a few hours tossing pebbles into Jamaica Bay. Over the past few weeks he had grown very familiar with this calm stretch of water that separated Queens from Brooklyn. It was a place he could enjoy his solitude and dream of a world filled with chances and hope rather than disappointments and closed doors. He would have stayed there forever except for the hungry gnawing in his gut that pushed him back toward Brooklyn. If he could just find an odd job, maybe he could eat his first hot meal in weeks.

As he strolled down the crowded streets, his dark eyes were down, avoiding the disparaging stares the city's respectable citizens tossed his way. Hearing the clanging of a bell, he shifted to the right just in time to avoid being hit by a streetcar. He then waited for a series of automobiles to chug by before ambling across Bergen Street. Standing on the curb, he considered what direction he would take next.

Across the street were the Bergen Street Stables. Wearing a dark suit, white shirt, and tie, a beefy, balding Mark Devin stood in the building's entry and stared out into the street. The world was a much different place than it had been a decade before when he'd built the stables. Then there had been no cars and now there were hundreds buzzing by each hour. While tens of thousands of horses still pulled wagons, they were slowly being replaced by trucks. Thus, things didn't look good for the long-term for his business.

His morning chores completed, Devin waved to a few shopkeepers and visited with a beat cop. The policeman pointed out the stranger leaning against the wall. Gallagher waited for the officer to move on before pushing off the wall and slowly making his way across the street. He paused for a second, smiled, and, when he was sure the man in the suit had seen him, mumbled, "Hi."

Devin immediately shot back, "Hello. You need someone, young man?"

Crossing his arms over his ragged suit coat, Gallagher nodded. "I need a job. Could you use someone?"

The visitor was a mess. His hair had not been cut in months. It was greasy and uncombed. The suit he wore was frayed and faded; dirt and oil spots ran up the pants legs. Though it was a warm day, the man's coat collar was buttoned indicating he likely didn't even own a shirt. His boots had holes in the toes and were caked with mud. His hands were dirty and his fingernails long. He looked more like a whipped dog than a man. The visual exam completed, Devin lifted his eyebrow, ran his hand across his smooth-shaven chin, and admitted, "I recently lost a man. I could use some help. Do you have any references?"

Gallagher looked down, shook his head, and remained sadly mute.

"What's your name?" Devin asked.

"Gallagher. I'm Thomas Gallagher."

"And where did you last work?"

The visitor looked up. For the first time his face revealed signs of hope. "I worked on the Pennsylvania Highway."

"Why aren't you still there?" the stable owner demanded.

"I just got tired of it," came the quick reply.

"You mean you got fired," Devin shot back.

There was no use lying; the man had Gallagher pegged. "I got fired, but not because I didn't do the work. It was because I wasn't union. I didn't have a card and had been using one I borrowed."

Devin shook his head, "You mean stole?"

The young man nodded, "But I had to eat. And I really am a good worker."

"Maybe you are and maybe you aren't," Devin acknowledged. "Let's go into the office. I got something to say that doesn't need to be heard on the street."

Devin led the dirty, smelly visitor into the stable and through a door into a small, well-kept room. After sitting behind a large oak desk, the businessman pointed to a wooden chair. Only when Gallagher was seated did the owner speak.

"Why were you in prison?"

"What do you mean?" the visitor replied.

"Don't deny it. Your clothes are what they issue men when they are released. You are an ex-con, so why were you behind bars?"

"Had no family," he whispered. "I stole to eat."

"If I give you a chance," Devin asked, "will I regret it?"

Pulling his head up and looking the older man squarely in the eyes Gallagher answered, "No, sir."

"OK," Devin said, "I'm going to give you an advance on your first week's wages. You get yourself a meal and some new clothes. Then you come back here and go to work." He paused before asking, "You got a place to stay?"

"No, sir," came the reply.

"Do you mind sleeping in the stable's hayloft?"

"Be the best place I've slept in a long time."

"OK," Devin replied, "I need someone to watch the place at night. So you have the job."

Devin's confidence in Gallagher proved out. He did the tough, dirty jobs and was gentle and compassionate with the horses. He worked hours without complaint and displayed no bad habits. And the young man seemed genuinely thrilled to have this second chance in life.

Perhaps because he had been hungry for so long, Gallagher saved whatever he could from his small weekly salary. He happily told the customers the cash was being put back so that he could buy a fine coat before January. He then explained he had never had a winter coat. Even as a child he suffered in the cold. If he could just own a heavy coat, then he would feel like a king.

November 25 brought snow and cold winds to Brooklyn. Gallagher wrapped himself in an old sweater and got up before dawn to start his work. By the time one of the other employees came in, the snow was several inches deep.

Milt Curran glanced over at Gallagher, "You eaten anything today?"

"Naw," the lanky man replied.

"Then why don't you walk down to the café and grab some breakfast. Things will be slow due to the weather. I can manage without you for a while."

Gallagher glanced out the door and into the near blizzard-like conditions. Snow was blowing almost sideways. "Not sure I want to get out in that mess."

"You better go now," Curran suggested, "it's only going to get worse. If you wait for lunch you might not be able to find anything open."

Though he hated facing a howling wind and temperature in the teens, Gallagher knew Curran was right. Pulling the sweater around his neck and yanking a hat over his head, he began the trek to the nearest diner. The young man hurriedly wolfed down flapjacks, bacon, and eggs. Knowing things were only going to get worse, he quickly took a last sip of hot coffee, paid for his meal, jammed the hat back on his head, walked out into the frigid air, lowered his head, pushed his hands into his pockets, and plowed through the foot-high drifts that now covered the sidewalk.

Getting to the café had been a spring walk in the park compared to the return trip to the stable. The wind had become a gale pushing the bitter air right through his clothes. He could barely breathe and the concrete was now so slick he fell several times in the first block. Crossing the almost vacant street, he stood under a storefront's overhang for a few moments, caught his breath, and then moved on.

As the wind picked up and the snow fell even harder, Gallagher found himself in an unexpected battle for survival. The cold was numbing as it roared into the deep recesses of his body. His cheekbones felt as though they were going to rip through his skin and his head throbbed. Fighting the gale, he stumbled along, and then fell, pushed up, shook off the snow, and fell again. The front of his body was so plastered with snow he looked like a slowly moving statue. The tears rushing from his eyes froze instantly on his cheeks. He could barely feel his hands and his feet were crying out in pain. Rounding a corner, the stiff breeze caught his hat, ripping it from his head and throwing it against a brick wall. Gasping in the cold air, he blindly turned and chased the rolling headgear for almost twenty feet before it came to rest in a three-foot drift that had formed against a warehouse wall. Bending over and grabbing the hat, he turned once more to face the storm. And then he heard a soft cry.

Gallagher rubbed the snow from his eyes and studied the ground. Something was in distress. What was it? Falling to his knees the ex con dipped his already frozen hands into the snow and started frantically digging. Two feet down he finally found the source of the weak whimpering.

As Gallagher picked the mutt up and dusted away the snow, he got a better read on the animal's condition. He was emaciated and trembling, his bones all but pushing through his coat. Except for a few black spots around his face, he was solid white. As the man drew the small pup closer something else became obvious. This dog hadn't been lost; it had been thrown away like a piece of trash. And the pup had been beaten too; judging by the wounds probably with a stick or board. It had been worked over so severely a tooth had been broken.

In light of the fact that the dog was more dead than alive, Gallagher should have moved on, gotten back to the stable, and out of the weather before he froze to death. Yet, as he studied the bundle of fur and bones he didn't see a dog; he saw himself. Like the dog, he had been abandoned. He had survived beatings too. And, he'd been thrown away as trash. So he couldn't leave the mutt on the streets. If it was going to die at least Gallagher wanted to assure the guy that someone on this planet cared.

Stuffing the tiny dog under his sweater, he turned back into the storm. Blinded by the snow and dizzy from exposure, the thin man pushed forward. He had a block to go and with new determination he ignored the stinging in his feet and the pain in his head. He fell several more times before he finally arrived, all but frozen, at the stable.

Charging into the barn, Gallagher looked over at Curran, "Never seen weather like this before."

"It's a big storm," the older man agreed. After he latched the door, Curran turned back to Gallagher just as the thin man pulled the pup from under his sweater. "What's that you got there?"

Sitting down on an overturned bucket, Gallagher shrugged, "Just a mutt someone tossed away. Poor little guy is in bad shape too. But I couldn't leave him out in the snow. What kind of man would I be if I did that?"

"What you going to do with it?" Curran asked as he closed the distance between them. "He kind of looks like a sorry excuse for a terrier."

"Try to save its life. If it lives then I guess I'll see if Mr. Devin will let him stay here with me."

Curran shrugged, "Let me get some blankets for you and that critter. Looks like you both need some warming up."

As Gallagher rubbed the ten-pound dog's body in an effort to get his circulation going, Curran went into the office to the building's only stove and poured a cup of coffee. He then quickly walked back into the stable and over to Gallagher, "Hold the cup in your hands and then rub down the dog. That might help him warm up more quickly. Now I'll get a couple of horse blankets."

Gallagher took a sip and then leaned down and dripped a bit of the hot coffee into the dog's mouth. The dog licked the liquid and cried out as if demanding more. A dozen sips later he had revived enough to stand on his thin, wobbly legs and take in his surroundings. As Gallagher reached forward to pick him up, the pup cowered and scooted away.

"He's been beaten," Curran noted as he handed his coworker a blanket.

"Yeah, somebody has worked him over real good," Gallagher

said. "And the way he's scared indicates he has been beaten a bunch of times."

"How would you know that?" Curran asked.

"I just know," Gallagher assured him. Reaching forward he pulled the frightened, hungry pup back to his side and wrapped a blanket around him. "Don't worry, little guy," he whispered, "nobody will ever beat you again."

"I know Mr. Devin doesn't like anyone in his office," Curran noted, "but as cold as it is, don't think he'd mind if you and the pup spent the rest of day and night in there. And I'll leave you some of the mutton I've got in my lunch box to feed him. Then I think I'll head home. Even though it's only a couple of blocks away, if I don't take off now I might not get there." The man grabbed his coat and grinned at the pup, "What you going to call him?"

"Same thing folks used to call me."

"What's that?"

"Bum," came the short reply.

For the next twenty-four hours Gallagher never let the tiny dog out of his sight. He kept him near as he did his chores and by his side as he bedded down for the night. Still, anytime he reached down to pick the dog up, the mutt trembled.

"Don't worry, boy, I'm not going to hit you." But even the soft words did little good. Bum had no trust of humans. Yet late that night, when Gallagher pulled the creature to his chest, the dog wagged its broken and mangled tail for the first time. The man smiled. The storm might have been still raging outside, but in the stable a man and a pup had found warmth and peace.

The next morning when Devin fought his way through

drifts to his business, Gallagher already had the horses fed, stalls cleaned, and was working on grooming a bay. Beside his feet sat the mangled little mutt, seemingly following the man's every move.

Devin smiled and shrugged, "Where did that come from?"

"Found him in a snow drift. He was all but dead."

"Doesn't look too good right now," the owner observed.

"He reminds me of me," Gallagher explained. "I was hoping you'd let me keep him."

Devin's blue eyes moved from the dog to the man and back to the dog. Crossing his arms just above his ample belly, he smiled, "Thomas, you know anything about the story of the Good Samaritan?"

"I've heard it," Gallagher admitted. "I think that is what you were to me?"

Devin shook his head, "Don't know about that, but I do know this. Over the past two months you have become the best worker I've ever had. I wish I could pay you more. Taking a chance on you was one of the wisest things I've ever done. So, if you think that pup needs a second chance then I'll trust your judgment."

"Thank you, sir," Gallagher replied. "You won't be sorry."

Over the next few weeks the former convict gave himself completely to the tiny dog. Dipping into his savings, Gallagher bought lean meat and bones from a local butcher. For the first few days he even handfed the abused creature. The hard work and special diet paid great dividends. By the middle of December, Bum had gained five pounds, but the dog's health came with a great price. As a harsh New York winter approached, Gallagher no longer had the money to buy a heavy coat. Still, he felt the pup's love and devotion might be enough to keep him warm on even the coldest days. Thankfully, the two outcasts had somehow found each other and in the process found an acceptance neither had ever known.

Though Bum was now completely devoted to the man who'd saved his life, he still trembled if someone else approached him. What had this poor creature been through before the stable hand discovered him in the blizzard? It would be a question no one could answer, but it was obvious the scars the dog carried were much deeper than the broken tooth and mangled tail.

Christmas Eve had been cold and clear and a strong breeze dropped the windchill down to just above zero. It was just past eight when Devin emerged from his office and strolled out into the main part of the stable. In his arms he held a dozen packages.

"You look like Santa Claus," Gallagher remarked, his voice a bit hoarse.

"When you have five children," Devin laughed, "you do have to play that role."

He had no more than finished his explanation than Gallagher began to cough. The deep hacking went on for several moments before the room again grew quiet.

"That is a wicked cough you have there," the businessman noted. "Are you all right?"

"I'm fine," Gallagher assured him.

Devin carefully eyed his worker, "It is really cold tonight, so be sure and cover the horses with blankets and add some extra straw to their bedding." He stopped for a moment and stepped closer to Gallagher, "Your face looks pale. You sure you're all right? I mean, that mutt looks better than you right now and Bum might be the ugliest dog in Brooklyn."

"Just a cold," Gallagher assured him, "and thanks for all you have done for me."

"I should be thanking you," Devin replied. "You deserve a raise and you'll be getting one at the first of the year. And, when you finish your chores tomorrow, come up to my house. I want you to have Christmas dinner with us. We'll serve the meal at two. Can you make it there by then?"

Gallagher coughed again. After clearing his throat he asked, "Are you sure you want me at your house?"

"You be there at two and you'll get the best Christmas meal you've ever tasted."

"I have no doubt it will be that."

Devin moved the packages to his right arm, reached into his pocket, and pulled out a five-dollar bill. He handed it to Gallagher and almost sang out, "Merry Christmas." As his shocked employee studied the bill, the older man headed out into the night to catch a streetcar to the other side of town. After his boss left, Gallagher carefully pushed the money into his pocket, bolted and locked the door, and went about his work. By the time he and Bum climbed into the loft the man was chilling with fever.

"I'm not going to be cold too much longer, Bum," he whispered. "The day after Christmas I'm going to use that five and buy myself a coat."

For the first time since the day he had found Bum, Gallagher couldn't get warm. Even piling extra horse blankets over his shivering body didn't help. And, as the hours passed, his deep cough grew worse. Unable to sleep, at 3:00 the man got up make sure the horses were warm. After checking their blankets and adding more straw in the stalls, he collapsed. As a curious horse looked down and Bum tugged at his shoe, Gallagher fought to get up. He couldn't; he was simply too weak.

As the minutes passed and his body began to shut down, the stable hand no longer felt the cold. Except for the noise out on the streets and the church bells ringing at dawn, he heard nothing. Finally, at about the time the Devin children were running downstairs to see what Santa had left them, Gallagher lapsed into unconsciousness.

As light began to filter through the windows, Bum licked the man's face. He didn't wake up. The dog then nosed the man's hand. Gallagher didn't stir. Only when the pup climbed back on the man's chest did he rouse and whisper, "You're a good dog, Bum." Then his voice again grew still.

When Bum was unable to wake his master again, the concerned dog bounded into the office. There was no one there. Racing to the front door, he jumped against it. It wouldn't budge. Running over to a window, the dog climbed up on a wooden crate and looked out. The window was locked as well.

Jumping down, he raced back to his master. Gallagher was still cold and unmoving. When the dog climbed on his chest, he didn't respond.

Bum had never been a barker. He had likely adopted that trait to keep from being beaten. Those who had visited the stable had remarked several times how nice it was to be around a quiet dog. So it must have taken every bit of courage the small animal could muster to run back to the window, start pawing at the glass, and howl. And once he started, he didn't quit.

Neighbors who were trying to celebrate Christmas quickly grew weary of the mutt's cries. Many opened their apartment doors to see where the noise was coming from. Others yelled out curses demanding the owner do something about the insistent animal. Five minutes became ten and ten became twenty, and Bum continued to cry as if his life depended upon it.

Pat Kittery put up with the racket for a half hour before grabbing his coat and stepping out into the cold air. From his home's steps he noted the noise appeared to be coming from the stable. Walking across the street, he saw Bum in the window. Approaching the glass he tapped it and said, "Be quiet." The dog barked even louder. Strolling around to the front, Kittery tried the door; it was locked. Sticking his hands into his pockets, he turned and made his way north. Milt Curran lived a few blocks down the street. He'd have a key to the stable and then the two of them could find out why the usually mute Bum was so excited.

Ten minutes later, with Bum still howling, Curran unlocked the door. The dog rushed up to him, his deformed tail wagging, and then ran back to an open horse stall. Kittery and Curran followed and discovered the unconscious Gallagher. He was as cold as ice and barely breathing. As Curran tried to revive his coworker, Kittery ran to a neighbor who had a phone. After placing a call to Devin, he hurried back to the barn. Curran had fired up the stove and carried Gallagher into the office. By the time a worried Devin arrived with a doctor, the weak man had opened his eyes.

"He'd have died today if you hadn't found him," the physician explained while looking up at Curran.

The man shrugged, "None of us were coming in today. Nobody would have found him if Bum hadn't raised such a ruckus. It's that dog that saved Gallagher's life."

"As soon as he is strong enough to move," Devin said, "we're taking him back to my house. That young man and this dog need a home. They've each proven themselves worthy of that and so much more. I don't know what I would have done if that boy had died."

Curran leaned over to Gallagher and whispered, "Your dog performed a miracle today."

"A Christmas miracle," the doctor added.

"And in a stable too," Devin noted.

As Bum dug his nose into Gallagher's cheek, the man smiled.

Gallagher never ran for political office or developed a miracle drug. He lived his life quietly in Brooklyn working in the stable. Bum never saved another life or grew to trust many people other than Gallagher. He remained a homely, shy dog who rarely barked. But what happened at the Bergen Street Stables on December 25, 1910 remained a part of Brooklyn lore for decades. The story of Gallagher and Bum is the American equivalent of Aesop's famous fable. And it is just as timeless—return kindness with kindness, love with love, and sacrifice with sacrifice and you fully understand the meaning of Christmas and the joy of earning a dog's devotion.

11

PURPOSE

★ ★ ★

DRIVEN TO GO BEYOND THE CALL

Efforts and courage are not enough
without purpose and direction.
—*John F. Kennedy*

December 7, 1941 changed everything. Before the attack on Pearl Harbor the United States had managed to stay out of a conflict that was raging across almost a third of the planet. Yet on that day of infamy, Japanese bombs woke up Americans to a reality that shook them to the core. We would be fighting a war on two fronts, against powerful enemies that were far better prepared and much more experienced than we were. Over the next few weeks millions were going to be called into military service and at the same time civilian life would dramatically be altered in ways people could not begin to imagine.

When the news filtered across radios to Pleasantville, New York, it was early afternoon. The community's history could be traced almost back to the new world's first settlers. It has survived British occupation during the American Revolution and, before the Civil War, was an important link in the Underground Railroad helping to transport escaped slaves from the south to Canada. Now in Pleasantville, talk of football, Broadway plays, and Christmas had been placed on the back burner. All that mattered was the war and what it meant to the town and the nation.

Edward J. Wren and his family were among those who called Pleasantville home, but on this horrific day the Wrens had no idea that what had just happened in Hawaii would change their world and dramatically impact the lives of two American generals. In fact, an adopted member of the family would set in motion a series of events that would even make waves in the halls of Congress.

Almost three years before, over Wren's better judgment, he had allowed his children to adopt an energetic mongrel puppy with large feet and an almost comedic curious expression. Within a year the dog had grown into his paws, reached more than fifty pounds, and destroyed everything from shoes to parts of the backyard. Chips, as the children named him, possessed two traits that the man of the house both admired and despised. The first was great energy. The dog simply never wore down. The second was an inexhaustible curiosity. Those two attributes combined to make the animal a great playmate for the children but also got him in constant trouble when he was left to his own devices.

The best anyone could tell, Chips's questionable lineage was a mix of shepherd, husky, and collie. In his face he looked like a shepherd but it was in his build the husky stood out. And when neighbors called complaining about the dog digging in their yards or chasing their cats, Wren sometimes wished he could send the dog off to Alaska to pull sleds and chase polar bears. Nevertheless, because his kids loved Chips, the businessman could not find good enough reasons to separate them from the big guy. Besides, it was very likely that no one else would have wanted the misfit anyway. Yet when America was plunged into war Wren discovered the country needed more than just men; the United States also was looking for large, agile dogs to fill roles in the military.

Spurred by a story he read in the *New York Times* on "Dogs for

Defense," Wren put a leash on Chips, took a trip downtown, and allowed the local army recruiters to check him out. The military officials liked both his size and alertness. His health was good as well. So within a few days the dog said goodbye to suburban life, was placed in a crate, loaded into a baggage car, and shipped to the War Dog Training Center at Front Royal, Virginia. At that time no one could have guessed that Chips was a hero in the making. Wren even wondered if the canine misfit wouldn't flunk out of basic training and be back home in a matter of weeks.

In early 1942, America and its military were still concerned with what was then called "fifth column assaults." There was a strong belief that the Axis powers had a sizeable and well-organized group that had been in the U.S. for many years. It was said that this group, disguised as normal citizens, was waiting for war to break out so they could stage attacks on everything from military bases and government offices to seacoast shipping facilities and war plants. Thus, there was a rush to train dogs not for work overseas as much as in protecting the home front from internal forces. So in those early days of World War II, most of the dogs that were "drafted" into service were being trained for sentry duty. Those in charge at Front Royal figured that was where Chips would end up as well. But, as would be revealed by his training, this mutt was unique. His ability to not just learn commands but also actually reason would quickly place him head and shoulders above most of the other dogs in canine boot camp.

During his basic training Chips was teamed with Private John Rowell. Because of his firm, but loving nature, Chips quickly bonded with the Arkansas native. That strong relationship built on trust was vital because, in the Virginia woods and across the state's streams and valleys, the routine established in this dog-training program was even more difficult and rigorous than human boot camp. Without dog and man working as a precise team, the animal would fail and be shipped back home.

In areas where Union and Confederate forces once staged bloody battles, Chips learned to climb under barbed wire, crawl on his belly for hundreds of yards, carry a pack, run away from grenades, endure the sounds of artillery, and silently swim across lakes. He was exposed to explosions and machine gun fire. He was taught to march in formation, jump over high fences, and ride almost motionless in trucks. He lived in extreme conditions, sleeping in the rain and cold, marching in the heat, and was taught to avoid any food except what Rowell offered to him. Over the weeks Chips easily endured the hardship, the long hours, and the intense training to learn all but one of the skills needed to graduate basic training. That final essential element the dog was required to embrace went against the very nature of the one-time family pet.

Chips, the dog that had been a nanny to the kids around his Pleasantville neighborhood, had to learn how to attack and fight. To earn his stripes he was expected to be aggressive, to challenge an enemy, and, on command, take him down. He was to continue tearing at the man until Rowell called him off. If that order did not come then Chips was to keep attacking until the "intruder" was dead.

Up until this point basic training had been a grand adventure. It was all about fun and games in the woods. But asking a family dog to become a trained killer was something very different. It simply was not a part of Chips's fiber. He didn't fully grasp the concept until one of the other men brutally knocked Rowell to the ground. Seeing the man who had been training him for weeks attacked brought out the instinct the army needed. The dog flew into a rage and attacked. He didn't stop his assault until a smiling Rowell pulled him off. The final question had been answered and the last bridge had been crossed: Chips had emerged from training as a finely tuned piece of U.S. Army machinery and could be used as a military sentry dog. There was one more test to measure if the dog was really something special. And, when faced with that test, leading his handler safely through a myriad of traps along a long agility course, Chips mastered every challenge and became the first dog to ever earn a perfect score. That A+ final grade meant Chips would not be guarding against fifth column assaults; he and his handler would be shipped overseas with the 3rd Infantry to fight on the African front.

The voyage over was a sobering one for those men getting ready for battle for the initial time. The conditions were cramped and there was little to do. Worst of all, there was too much time to think about what they were leaving behind and what they might face ahead. There was also a constant fear of a German U-boat spotting the ship and launching torpedoes.

While the soldiers worried, for Chips the voyage was just another new adventure. After months of hard training it was as if he was suddenly on vacation. He got to walk on the deck, watch the ocean, observe poker games, and listen to men sing. Yet what was about to greet him in Africa was far different than anything the dog had experienced in New York or Virginia.

Thanks to the movie *Casablanca,* Americans were well aware of the Nazi occupation in North Africa. The 3rd was expected to help the British deal with Frenchmen who had worked with Hitler's forces as well as to drive the Germans out of the area. Battling heat, sand, and aggressive resistance, the months spent in Africa saw the new recruits face some of the toughest conditions of the war. The desert and its temperature extremes offered unique challenges like nothing they had known in boot camp, but the actual fighting was not as bloody as anticipated. The enemy had less will than expected.

As the sounds of battles raged in the distance, Chips stood his ground miles away from danger. His job was to guard tanks, and most of the folks he saw were members of the Allied forces. Chips might as well have been in Pleasantville. His army training wasn't doing much good in a place where the front lines were miles away. At this point there were no signs that this member of the K-9 Corps would ever distinguish himself in combat much less become a national hero.

As they waited well behind the lines, Rowell and Chips were always together. As per army regulations, the dog was beside the man when he ate, played cards, or wrote letters home. At this point those notes to Rowell's family and friends carried little news of a war that for the moment was going well and mainly described the harsh environment and sandy terrain that was so different from his native Arkansas.

When the Axis powers were driven out of Africa in the early summer, the 3rd was sent to chase them. This time what faced the Americans would be much different than what they had experienced during their first encounters with the enemy. Hitler was not going to give up Europe without tossing everything he had at the Allies.

Rowell and his company had been attached to the 7th Army under the command of George S. Patton. Moving into the next stage of combat with the Yanks were members of the British 8th Army and a group of Canadian infantry. The men were briefed on what was ahead, and Patton assured them there would be no turning back. The only possible outcome was either victory or death, and they should be prepared for both.

Leaving North Africa, the 3rd boarded a ship and took a route north across the Mediterranean Sea. While Rowell cleaned his gun and readied for combat, a bored Chips rested. This time things just felt different. As the man silently considered what was in front of him, he sensed there would be no easy road from here on in. The long fight had started and many of those around them today likely wouldn't be around when the war was finally over.

In the early morning of July 10, 1943, Allied forces rushed ashore just east of Licata on the southern coast of Sicily. They faced tough enemy resistance. Waiting on a landing craft just off the coast and out of the range of fire, Private Rowell detected the sights of battle at dawn. The Arkansas native observed the flash of grenades and mortar fire, the sound of rifles and machine guns, and bursts of yellow and orange flame all along the beach. At times the skies lit up with massive explosions, and in the distance men cried out for help in a number of different languages. Soon the smell of gunpowder crossed the waters and stung his nose. Looking down to his side, Rowell noted the dog shaking his big, dark head and pawing at his muzzle. He smelled it too.

Sitting down the man steadied his nerves by stroking Chips's back. As he considered his first step into real war, he thought back to Virginia. This was what they had trained for and for the first time the two of them were about to find out what they were made of. And Chips was the best of the best; because of his skills and instincts this athletic dog was here rather than guarding the gate at some stateside base. So going into battle Rowell couldn't ask for a better soldier watching his back.

As shells exploded overhead and the craft grew closer to the shore, Chips seemed focused and ready. It was as if the dog understood this was not an exercise; it was war. The bullets fired would be real and men were going to die. In fact, as he heard the screams in the background, the dog likely sensed some of those soldiers he knew had already paid the price required of this fight. Yet, even while men around him trembled and others frantically mumbled prayers, Chips was not agitated. As he studied his charge, Rowell would later swear that he saw purpose in the dog's deep brown eyes.

"Get ready," one of the officers yelled over the noise as the craft drew closer to the shore.

Getting up and crouching down in the craft, his gun in hand, Rowell took a deep breath, thought once again of his family and the hills of home, grabbed his dog's lead, and looked toward the front of the boat. Chips rose to his feet and stood beside Rowell. His short, thick coat bristled and his mouth opened slightly, his tongue dropping out on the left side. Now it was just a matter of waiting for the landing vessel to hit the coast and the door to drop.

The boat shook violently and a second later the entry swung open. Charging out into fire, Rowell and Chips raced through the water and hit the beach. Surprisingly, there was little resistance. As they crawled over the damp sand, passing the bodies of men who had been a part of an earlier landing, they were met with only scattered fire. For a moment Rowell and the members of his band thought they had gotten lucky.

The almost confused soldiers paused, looked at each other, then back to their commander. Receiving the order to drop down and move slowly, they crept forward. Crawling beside them, his lead firmly in Rowell's hand, was Chips. Just like the men in his company, the dog's eyes were darting side to side as if trying to figure out what this new experience had to offer. Still, meeting no resistance, Rowell and his comrades relaxed. It appeared that for them the war had been postponed for another day. Yet just as the soldiers grinned at one another, Chips's shoulders tensed. Laying his muzzle on his paws, he fixated on a small, seemingly vacant hut barely more than a hundred feet ahead.

"What is it, boy?" Rowell whispered.

The dog lifted his head and sniffed the air. The trainer was sure the dog detected something, but what? There was no enemy in sight.

Just as the Arkansan and the others in his landing party pushed off their bellies to stand, blasts of continuous fire rang out. Hitting the sand and rolling over, Rowell glanced back to the hut. The enemy was hiding a machine gun nest inside that fisherman's tiny shack.

The gunfire was now intense and the American soldiers were trapped in the open with nowhere to hide. With no help to either side, he and his companions were sitting ducks. As rounds kicked up sand all around him, Rowell pushed even closer to the ground. The emplacement was too far away to reach with a thrown hand grenade, and the enemy was too well hidden to be taken out with rifle fire. In the game that was war, it appeared that the Americans were holding the losing hand.

In the panic caused by walking into a death trap, the dog trainer had all but forgotten about Chips. Turning his head to the right, he reached his hand out to pat his friend. When his hand met the big dog's head, Chips snarled, rolled away, jerked the leash from Rowell's hand, and leapt to his feet.

"Chips, halt!"

The dog ignored the man's order. His dark eyes glowing in the early morning sun, he dug his claws into the sand and shot across the open ground toward the hut. The enemy must have noticed the quickly advancing member of the K-9 Corps because they redirected their fire in his direction. But they reacted a bit too slowly. As the Americans helplessly looked on, Chips raced just in front of the fire and toward the nest. Within seconds he arrived at his objective, burst through a side door, and into the hut.

The dog found himself facing a quartet of Italian soldiers. Rather than choose one to punish for shooting at his trainer, Chips charged at all four men, driving them back against a far wall, in the process knocking the machine gun from its stand. Sensing the dog was a real threat, one of the men drew a pistol from his belt and took aim. Rather than back off, Chips charged him, yanking his wrist to the side. When the weapon discharged it creased the dog's skull but didn't slow him down. Knocking this shooter off his feet, the angry canine turned his attention to another. Yelping and growling, the seemingly deranged four-legged warrior sank his teeth into the Italian's leg knocking him to the ground.

Sensing he was facing a force for which he had no answers, the man who had been firing the machine gun opted not to challenge the angry beast. Turning, he attempted to retreat out the door. Just as he made his way to the entry, Chips jumped forward clamping his mouth down on the man's throat. Trying to yank the animal from his neck, the man staggered out into the open and fell on the ground.

As soon as the members of the 3rd saw Chips wrestling with the Italian, they pushed off the ground and sprinted to the hut. As Rowell held his gun on the man the dog had grabbed, two other Americans rushed into the hut. There they found three enemy soldiers who had already tossed down their weapons and had their hands over their heads. With ripped uniforms and bleeding wounds, all three also exhibited signs of having experienced the extreme wrath of the angry American dog.

Rowell allowed Chips to punish the other outmanned captive for only a few more seconds before ordering the dog to retreat. Growling, the canine opened his jaws, licked his lips, and backed up to his trainer while never once taking his eyes off the frightened Italian. It was only then Rowell noted that Chips was bleeding from a bullet wound at the top of his skull and had powder burns in several different places on his head and body. Turning back to the troops who were now approaching, Rowell yelled for a corpsman.

The company medic quickly evaluated the dog's injuries, cleaned the wounds, and assured a concerned Rowell that Chips was fit for duty. Not sending the dog back to a field hospital put the canine into position to once again save the lives of the men in his company.

Late that evening it seemed apparent that the Italians were on the run. There was so little actual fighting in the area that the Americans were told to set up camp along the beach and catch some sleep. As Rowell tried to get comfortable, Chips, sporting a bandage on his head, lay down beside him and drifted into a restless slumber. It didn't last long.

During the night, the dog awoke and sat up. Remaining mute, he leaned forward and nosed his trainer's face. Opening his eyes, Rowell noted the dog's tense manner and bristling coat. Grabbing his rifle and rolling over, the private came to his feet and silently nudged his comrades. When the men questioned what was going on, Rowell urged them to keep quiet and pointed to the dog.

With a dozen men now awake and ready for action, Chips led the way toward the beach. In the moonlight the Americans saw what the dog had sensed. Ten Italian soldiers were sneaking up a trail to stage a surprise attack. Thanks to the dog's advance warning, the G.I.s silently closed in behind the enemy. Without having to fire a single shot the men from the 3rd were able to easily apprehend and disarm the Italians. With Chips nipping at their heels, the enemy was then marched into the camp to be shipped off to a prisoner of war camp.

Captain Edward G. Parr noted Chips's actions that night and recommended the U.S. Army give the dog a citation for "single-handedly eliminating a dangerous machine gun nest and causing the surrender of its crew." He also suggested this member of the K-9 Corps should receive a Purple Heart for the injuries he sustained in the mission. Military regulations did not allow presenting a medal of any kind to what was considered a "piece of equipment," but Major General Lucian K. Truscott Jr., Commander of the 3rd, ignored those rules. Several months later, while on duty in Italy with a group of enlisted men and officers standing at attention, Chips was awarded the Distinguished Service Cross and the Purple Heart.

The dog was unimpressed with the awards but when newspapers ran the story in the States, William Thomas, who was the national commander of the Military Order of the Purple Heart, was outraged. He wrote letters to the president, the secretary of war, and the adjutant general of the United States Army demanding the awards be rescinded. He argued the dog was a tool and his injuries were no different than a Jeep being damaged in combat. In one of the strangest debates during the war, Congress spent three months trying to figure out what to do. They finally came to a compromise stating that while no medals designated for humans could be awarded to war dogs, other citations could be designed for that purpose. Thus, Chips would be the first and only canine to claim either the Distinguished Service Cross or the Purple Heart.

In the course of his career, the first dog hero of World War II served in Africa, Sicily, Italy, France, and Germany. Between combat duties, he was assigned to guard President Franklin Roosevelt and English Prime Minister Winston Churchill while they conferred at Casablanca. He also had the distinction of being the only member of the American military to attack General Dwight D. Eisenhower. It seemed Ike forgot that members of the K-9 Corps were taught to react to all strangers with great suspicion. When the general reached down to casually pet the four-footed hero, Chips did what he was taught to do and bit the man who had just saluted him. It took an order from his trainer before the dog let go of the right hand of the commander of the Allied Forces in Europe. The *New York Times* reported the encounter this way. "Chips, three-years-old, had already met Mr. Churchill and General Eisenhower and was anxious to bite Hitler too." Sadly, the dog never got that chance.

As the war drew to a close, Chips was with Rowell when the 3rd freed survivors of a concentration camp. Overseeing this sad scene and guarding the Germans who manned this horrible and inhuman outpost would be the dog's final duty before returning home.

War had taken a toll on the dog. The injuries he received in service had aged him both physically and mentally. Back in the States, Chips was deemed too weak to continue in military service. The Wrens were contacted and asked if they wanted to welcome the war hero back to their home in Pleasantville. Without hesitation they opened their doors and hearts to their old friend. This time the dog was no problem. Chips no longer chased the neighborhood cats or dug under fences. He didn't play with the kids either. It seemed he had left his heart and all of his energy on the war front in Europe. Without a task or a purpose, without John Rowell to protect, he had no zest for life. One night, after wearily looking at his New York yard for a final time, he went to sleep and never woke up. So like so many who served in the United States military, this hero died in obscurity with few realizing that he had given his soul and life for his country. But the men of 3rd Company never forgot the dog, and neither did a man named Ike.

12

CHARACTER

★ ★ ★

NOT JUST PLAYING A HERO

*Character cannot be developed in ease and quiet. Only through
experience of trial and suffering can the soul be strengthened,
ambition inspired, and success achieved.*
—Helen Keller

It was the summer of 1955 and the nation was going through a remarkable period of change. A world war had ended more than a decade before, television was replacing radio as the country's favorite entertainment source, the Korean conflict was now in the rearview mirror, and it seemed everyone liked Ike and the United States had emerged as the most powerful nation in the world. America's influence was stamped on everything from automobiles to music to fashion. When the people wanted new technologies or ideas, they looked to the U.S. The country's citizens were filled with such great optimism that most believed as good as things were, the best was yet to come.

Located more than twenty miles off the California coast, Santa Catalina Island had long been a playground for the wealthy and had become a postwar vacation hot spot for the growing middle class too. The rocky, twenty-two miles long island was home to just over two thousand residents, but on many days the population bloated to three and four times that amount. Largely owned by Chicago's famous Wrigley family and most often called "Catalina" by locals and tourists, the mere mention of its exotic name triggered thoughts of dynamic ocean views, fancy lodgings, great restaurants, and incredible fishing.

On this day three men traveled to the island to try their luck with rods and reels. Bringing along the latest in fishing equipment, the trio rented a small boat, cast off from shore, and motored out to sea. As the group only planned to be gone a few hours, they saw no reason to bring along any food or water. They also had no radio. But what could go wrong? This was America, and living life on the edge and believing the best would always happen meant there was no need for backup plans.

Initially the trip was everything they could have hoped for and more. It was a picture postcard kind of day. The seas were calm and their ride gentle. The views of the island from the ocean also brought a new perspective of the magnificence of the magical vacation spot. Large fish leaping from beneath the water and jumping over the waves indicated the men were in for a good afternoon of fishing too. On instinct, and against the advice they had been given before they had left the island, they pushed the boat further to the west figuring that even larger fish could be found in the waters few visited. Soon Catalina had all but disappeared and the Pacific surrounded them on all sides.

Cutting off the motor, the trio baited their hooks and cast their lines out into the exquisite blue water. They assumed they would get tired from yanking in their catch. Yet while they might have seen a lot of fish while motoring out to this spot, the prey had no interest in the lures the men were using. Hours went by without so much as a nibble. While the fishing had proven to be a wasted effort, the trio had nevertheless had a great time talking about everything from baseball to their families. It was a day they were sure they would never forget. As they fired up the motor to return to the dock, their optimistic view took a radical turn.

When the small boat's outboard motor first cut out, John

thought nothing of it. He knew they had plenty of gas and, as the engine had been running so smoothly all day, he figured perhaps a bit of dirt had gotten caught in the fuel line. As Jim and Bob looked on, John went to work dissecting the issue. Freeing up the supply line, he noted gas was still flowing freely. Putting things back together, he again tried to restart the engine. Though he wore himself out yanking on the pull rope, the motor didn't even cough.

John looked up at his friends and shrugged. Still, as the engine had run so well earlier, none of them was too concerned. They opted to let it sit for a while, figuring it might be flooded. As they looked back to the east they continued to make small talk, but this time there was a worried edge in their voices as each of them constantly glanced from the ocean back to the motor as if just staring at it might make it run.

After letting the gas drain from the carburetor for almost a half hour, John primed the engine and tried again. When he wore out, the other men gave it their best college efforts. When their combined attempts produced not even a weak sputter, they used wire pliers from their tackle box and removed the spark plug. Upon initial observation it looked fine; still, they cleaned the contact point with the blade of a knife and reinstalled it. It did no good. The trio then poured gas directly into the carburetor. Even though all three yanked on the starter string until they were covered in sweat, it was to no avail. The motor had given up the ghost. All that was left was to perform last rites. The problem was that without that engine they might well also be facing death.

A few hours before, they had shared the area with several boats. Now they were all alone on the high seas. Worse yet, it was less than an hour before sunset, and clouds were rolling in. As his now worried friends looked on, John continued to tinker with the engine. Yet, even after an hour of work the motor remained mute. As darkness set in, a blanket of fog rolled toward the boat. Soon the men could see no more than a few feet to each side and the current was carrying them further away from Catalina Island and safety.

"What are we going to do?" Bob asked.

John had no answer, but rather than admit the worst he simply smiled and assured his friends that someone would come along soon and tow them back to shore. Yet as the minutes ticked by and the only sound was the waves lapping against the wooden boat, it became impossible for even the calm war veteran to mask his apprehension. With the blanket of fog now completely covering the ocean, it was likely that no one would find them tonight. The longer they went without being spotted the longer were their odds of survival. In truth, as far as they were from the island, it might be days before someone happened onto them. With no other options, they once again baited their hooks and tossed their lines in the water. Yet as the fog grew thicker and as their boat steadily moved out deep into the Pacific, catching a big fish was the last thing on their minds.

Each of them knew the area history well enough to cite several stories of people who drifted out to sea without provisions. Some were never spotted again while others suffered for days without food and water before someone finally found them. Neither of those outcomes offered much hope for this adventure ending soon. Maybe that was why, just before they were immersed in complete darkness, John gave the motor another shot. He reset the choke, pulled the cord, and prayed. His prayers were not answered. The motor also didn't respond to the verbal abuse that followed. Thirsty and tired, he slumped back down in the tiny vessel and shook his head.

As the night set in the men began to voice their mistakes. The first was bringing a craft better suited for a lake or river. The next was leaving the island without provisions. And finally they should have never traveled so far away from Catalina. Now it was too late to correct any of those errors, and beating themselves up seemed an act of futility. What they needed was a plan and, like food and water, it was just another thing they didn't have.

Up until this point, the men had held on to their masculine pride. They had not resorted to crying out for help. Yet with all other options exhausted, first John, and then Bob and Jim, began to shout out into the darkness hoping against hope that someone might just hear.

Just a few miles away another boat was also drifting in the darkness. The middle-aged man who owned this small vessel was comfortable in the fog. He had provisions and thus saw no reason to fire up his engine and blindly try to make his way back to Catalina. In truth, with his demanding work schedule, he embraced this night on the water as an answered prayer. He was finally getting away from phone calls, meetings, and interviews. For the moment, as he enjoyed the solitude, he was perfectly content to bed down and wait for the weather to pass.

Looking toward the old dog resting on his deck, Rudd could not believe his good fortune. He had struggled for years carving out a living in motion pictures. During that time he had worked with some of the greatest stars in history. Many, such as John

Wayne, Humphrey Bogart, and Roy Rogers, had become his close friends. A host of other legends looked at Rudd's contributions to their movies in awe. But toward the early fifties the movie industry changed. The studio where he had spent a couple of decades no longer was interested in his services. Unable to make ends meet simply working for the movie industry, Rudd crossed over into television. Teaming with a friend, he'd become a part owner of a series on CBS. Thanks in large part to his imaginative contributions and a great team of writers and actors, the show became an overnight success. It had reopened doors Rudd figured would always be closed as well as giving him and his family a living that was far beyond his dreams. In a very real sense, he felt blessed. And this small but top-of-the-line vessel was a product of that success. It was a sign that the now almost fifty-year-old, solidly built, gray-haired man had beaten the odds. He doubted his time back on the top would continue for too long, but it was certainly sweet while it lasted.

The collie that slept a few feet from him had been there through all the good times and a few of the lean years. Wherever Rudd had gone, Pal had been at his side. Though his mahogany coat was not as thick as it once had been and the old guy's eyes didn't see like they had a decade before, he remained a remarkable animal. Though slowed by arthritis, he still ran in the fields, did tricks for family and friends, and chased motorcycles. But what Pal loved more than anything else was spending time with Rudd. Whenever the two were separated, the dog mourned. Thus the man even took the dog to work each day.

Rudd had never intended on owning a collie. He was more of a German shepherd kind of guy. He also liked little dogs that combined great energy with boundless curiosity. When Pal had fallen into his hands almost fourteen years before, Rudd worked with the pup for a few months before giving him to a friend who owned a ranch. But a few months later Rudd asked if he could have the collie back. When Pal returned, Rudd's luck dramatically changed. It was almost as if his success depended upon the dog.

Over the years the collie had learned close to three hundred different commands. But it wasn't just his intelligence that endeared him to the man. There was something about Pal's spirit that was unlike any dog he'd ever known; nothing could keep Pal down or hold him back. The collie remarkably understood Rudd and anticipated his needs. He'd bring the man everything from cigarettes to a newspaper without Rudd even asking for them. Rudd was therefore convinced that no matter how many other dogs he owned, there would never be another like Pal.

Yawning, the man stopped admiring his companion, got up from his chair, stretched, and walked over to take a final look at the fog rolling across the ocean. The dog moved beside him and almost by reflex Rudd patted the animal's head.

"Time for bed," he announced as he turned back to the boat's wheel. The dog, its attention still focused on the sea, didn't follow. Rudd twisted his neck and studied Pal for a moment before moving out of the damp air and to his bunk. The dog would join him when he was ready. Rudd had just drifted off to sleep when Pal began barking. The man lay in bed for several minutes, figuring whatever had upset his companion would soon pass, but when the noise continued he cried out the command to be quiet. For the first time in years, Pal ignored him.

Giving up, Rudd got out of bed and moved back to the side of the boat. The dog stopped barking. Staring out in the direction where the dog's nose pointed, the man saw nothing. Standing mute, he also heard nothing. Leaning down, he studied the collie. Pal was agitated; his face framed by what looked like a worried expression. Perhaps it was the fog or maybe the water lapping against the boat, but something had him spooked. Thus, rather than head immediately back to bed, Rudd sat down on the deck in hopes his presence would calm the dog. It didn't. Within seconds Pal was back at the side of the boat howling and barking as if a sea monster was about to leap out of the water and attack them.

For the next few minutes Rudd spoke soothing words to the collie. Pal didn't respond to them. He also didn't react to the order to shut up. But from time to time he would move up to another part of the boat, cock his ears, and listen. He was definitely hearing something, but what? Or maybe there wasn't anything to hear. Perhaps the old dog, already a couple years beyond the normal life expectancy of a collie, was losing touch with reality. Rudd had seen it happen with other senior dogs. As they aged their minds played tricks on them and they began to see and hear things that weren't there. A burst of fear and sadness rushed into the man's heart as he considered that his Pal might well be nearly at the end. He couldn't bear to think of life without the dog.

Across an expanse of ocean, the trio had given up on a miracle. Though none of them spoke of their fears, a sense of panic was setting in. At best they were going to spend a long night on the ocean, at worst they might drift for days. The frustrated men were tired and hungry, but what was really getting to them was their thirst. They were surrounded by water and trapped inside a moist bank of fog and yet they had nothing to drink.

They had cried out for help for more than an hour before their dry throats demanded they stop. Resting with their elbows on their knees and their heads in their hands, they looked more like mute statues than men. Their downcast expressions clearly reflected their moods. In their minds they were getting closer to a place from which there was no return. Consumed by pessimism likely magnified by the darkness, they began to voice their concerns as to how their families would handle it if their bodies were never found. They were still considering this sobering outcome when they heard a dog barking somewhere in the night.

With renewed hope they sat up. Had they somehow drifted toward shore rather than away from it? That went against the laws of physics, so it had to be something else. But what? Perhaps there was another boat out there. If that was the case, then they had to once more find their voices.

With much more emotion and enthusiasm than they had displayed earlier, they shouted out over the water and through the fog. They were banking all their hopes on the dog somehow hearing them and then finding a way to get a human to understand their plight. In a sense, that sounded crazy. The only time something like that happened was on a TV episode of *Lassie*. More than likely whoever owned the dog was going to scold it until it shut up. But as this seemed to be their only chance, they had to try.

More than a mile away, Rudd was tired of Pal's barking and ordered the dog to hush. But the collie again refused and the man walked up toward the front of the boat where his companion was staring out into the fog. For a few seconds, Rudd being at his side seemed to soothe Pal. Yet just when he thought the dog was ready to calm down, it began barking again. What could it be? After a minute of nonstop yelping, the dog hushed and everything was once again silent. Shaking his head, Rudd was about to force the collie back into the bow when he heard something that sounded like a man's voice. Where had it come from? As the dog and man remained mute, a man's plea for help came faintly again across the waves.

Feeling a need to apologize to his old friend, Rudd softly whispered, "Good boy." He then called out, "I hear you. Are you in trouble?"

A few moments later his question was answered, "Our motor is out. We are drifting. Can you help us?"

Rudd could not tell from which direction the voice was coming, so he was not sure where to go. And because of the fog he couldn't see more than a few feet in front of the boat. If he fired up the engine and headed out he might go in the wrong direction. Then he would lose contact with the helpless men. If they both just drifted perhaps he could stay in touch with them until the fog cleared. But what if the current took them in slightly different directions? Then he might never find them.

"I can't tell where you are," Rudd shouted.

"Please help us," another voice yelled back.

Were they ahead or to the side? They might even be behind him. Rudd simply didn't know. As he considered his limited options, he looked up to Pal. The dog's nose was pointing straight over the bow. Could the collie actually guide him to the other boat?

Calling back over the waves, Rudd said, "I'm going to fire up my motor and try to find you. Please keep yelling. I'll shut the engine off every so often to check if we are closer together." Rudd looked at his dog and added, "It is up to you. You have to guide me, boy."

Turning the key and pulling the choke, the man pushed the boat forward. At barely a crawl, he kept his eyes on his dog. Whenever Pal would move toward him he'd turn in that direction and wouldn't straighten up until the dog was back at the front of bow. In a sense he was using the collie as a compass. After a few minutes he cut the engine off.

"You out there?" Rudd yelled.

"Yes," came the reply.

They were closer. That had to mean Pal could hear or perhaps smell them even with the motor running.

"OK," Rudd called back. "Keep yelling!"

Over the course of the next thirty minutes, with the dog guiding him each step of the way, Rudd inched forward. He repeatedly cut off the engine, communicated with the men, then continued his journey. Finally, he could hear them as if they were next door. With Pal still barking he finally grew close enough to spot the stranded trio.

Cutting the motor, Rudd tossed the men a line and within minutes all three were out of their boat and had joined the man and his dog. After sharing some food and drink, the men told their story. Rudd then related the way the collie had guided him to them. With the fog now breaking up enough to travel, the boat was fired up and the quartet and the canine headed back to the island. This time the trip was uneventful.

Rudd dropped the trio and their small craft off at their dock. They thanked him once again and laughingly called his dog a "real-life Lassie." Without getting their names or sharing his own, he shook the trio's hands and headed to where he normally docked. After grabbing some sleep and eating breakfast, he and Pal traveled back to Los Angeles.

The next week Rudd was surprised when he received a telephone call while on the set of his television show. On the other end of the line was a representative of the Coast Guard. The man wanted to verify a story of life-saving effort by a man and his dog. The locals around Catalina thought the rescued men were describing Rudd and his collie. Still not sure what all the fuss was about, Rudd assured him the story was accurate but that it was really not a big deal. After verifying where the trio had been picked up, the Coast Guard officer explained that what had transpired was almost a miracle. The direction in which the men were drifting meant they might have never been spotted if the dog had not heard them that night. And because no one knew where to look for them, it was likely it would have been days before they had been reported missing, so they might never have been found.

Once again Rudd laughed it off. He assured the officer that the dog deserved all the credit and he should get none. He was just glad the men were all right. And that is when the Coast Guard official dropped the bombshell. The military organization wanted to present Pal with the Coast Guard's Certificate of Honor. They also requested they be allowed to use Pal's stage name on the award.

A few weeks later Rudd and Pal were given the tribute signifying the duo had come to the aid of three men whose lives were in danger. While the dog couldn't figure out what all the fuss was about and his owner didn't think what they had done deserved their being called heroes, they nevertheless accepted the award. But as Rudd looked down at the remarkable collie, he smiled. Perhaps it was fitting that Pal ended his career on this special note.

Though the men who were saved that night didn't realize it, Rudd Weatherwax had been training dogs to perform like heroes in the movies and on television for three decades. The dog that refused to quit barking and then guided the trainer to the stranded fishermen was his biggest star. Pal had played Lassie in the blockbuster hit film *Lassie Come Home*. Headlining in five more MGM movies, Pal would charm so many hearts, thrill so many audiences, and sell so many tickets he became one of the biggest box office stars in Hollywood. At the age of fourteen he would star in the pilot for the television series *Lassie*. When the network picked up the show, his son would take over the role and Pal retired, still on top of his game.

Even to this day the legacy that Pal initiated with his incredible abilities as a canine performer continues in new generations of collies bred from the same line. When Rudd died, his son Robert picked up the role as trainer. Hundreds of television shows and a dozen movies featuring Pal and his descendants have cemented Lassie's place as the world's most famous canine icon. Now, thanks to classic movie channels like TCM, worldwide television syndication, and DVDs, Pal is best remembered for his acting out the actions of Hollywood scriptwriters. What has been all but forgotten is the night the dog went off script in order to save three lives. What he did on that foggy evening proved the once unwanted collie was not just good at playing heroes; he also knew how to be one.

13

FAITHFULNESS

★ ★ ★

FINDING A CALLING

Success certainly isn't an achievement of popularity. Success in God's kingdom is loving God, loving one another, and being faithful to what He's called us to do.
—Gabriel Wilson

I opened the book talking about a dog's need to serve. Simply put canines are by nature not takers but givers. They want to earn their way and they need a calling to reach their full potential. And in some cases, if people don't present them with that calling, dogs will find it on their own. That is just what a collie-shepherd mix did in Moss Point, Mississippi, in 1952.

When Lulubelle was just six weeks old, one of Hugh Hern's coworkers at the International Paper Company knocked on the front door of the family's very modest frame home. Even before she noticed he had something in his hands, Hugh's wife, Wilma, invited the man into the house. The visitor ignored Hugh and the couple's elementary school-aged son, George, and hurried over to a six-month-old girl playing on an old quilt that had been placed on the floor. As a window fan battled the Gulf Coast summer heat and humidity, the toddler looked up, her big eyes questioning what the large, muscular man was doing invading her space. Pushing her rag doll to one side, the man opened his hands to reveal a tiny bundle of sable, black, and white fur topped with a wet, pink nose. Yvonne took one look at the puppy and giggled.

After the visitor set the pup on the floor, the tiny blonde girl reached out and gently stroked its tiny head. That simple gesture started the mutt's tail wagging. Within seconds the room was alive with yelps and laughs. Even if there was no camera, it was a Kodak moment—only rather than captured on film, it was deeply imprinted onto the minds of all there to witness this unique bonding of child and puppy.

As hard it might be for many today to believe, in 1952 many American families still didn't have a car. When they went someplace they used their feet. The Herns literally walked everywhere. That is the way the family went to church, shopping, or to the park. It was also the way George went to school and Wilma ran errands. About the only one who didn't usually walk was Hugh, who rode a bike to his job at International Paper.

The Herns also didn't have a television or air conditioning. They rarely went to movies or out to eat. Their lives were simple and uncluttered. And perhaps that is the reason Yvonne and Lulubelle were usually together. The dog was the little girl's playmate, confidant, and best friend. The mutt entertained the girl as well as served as her pillow for naps. They were practically inseparable. Even as a toddler Yvonne would horrify her mother by crawling under the house with the dog to escape the oppressive Mississippi heat. As usual, the two were together on an early fall morning when Lulubelle's calling would be triggered by Hugh's failing to complete a routine act.

George had already left for school when Hugh kissed Wilma goodbye, grabbed his bike, opened the gate, and left for his job. He was in such a hurry that he failed to notice the fence gate had not latched when he swung it shut. While the father might have missed that small point, his curious daughter did not. Sitting on the porch with Lulubelle, she spied the gate swing open. Getting up, she climbed down the steps to check it out.

Wilma Hern had no reason to ever worry about the daughter who spent much of each day playing outside. There was a fence all the way around the yard and the child was too small to climb over it. Besides, Lulubelle was the best babysitter in the world. If anything were wrong outside, she would surely alert Wilma.

Dressed in a frilly dress, white socks, and dark shoes, Yvonne strolled out to the gate and looked down the street. As the kids were all at school, everything was quiet and peaceful. While an inquisitive Lulubelle looked on, the child glanced back at the house and then marched through the gate. Making a left, she headed in the direction her brother went each day when he left for school.

On this sunny morning the child's course was anything but direct. While she had strolled the street many times with her mother, she'd never gotten to explore it on her own. So she stopped a half dozen times to study everything from fall flowers to birds in trees. Yet at no time did she ever consider turning around and going home. That thought never crossed her mind.

Lulubelle stuck by the tiny tot's right side, shadowing her every move, and keeping on the sidewalk and away from the street. For the dog this trip into the world was a new adventure, but she seemed to have a much better understanding of the dangers that lurked all around. Keeping her head low, she nervously glanced from side to side as she accompanied the little girl she dearly loved.

At the end of the first block was a highway filled with traffic. Even older elementary students were not allowed to cross the road without the aid of a school guard. Now, after all the kids were safely in class, there was no need for a person to wait at the corner to make sure children were safe.

Yvonne was so intently studying something on the other side of the highway that she failed to notice someone on the porch of a nearby home calling out to her. The woman yelling at the child was an invalid, confined to a wheelchair, and therefore seemingly helpless to stop what she knew was about to happen. As the girl drew closer to traffic, the woman cursed her inability to walk. Panic stricken, she was sure that the little girl's life could now be measured in seconds.

While not bumper-to-bumper, the road was busy. Cars and trucks were racing in both directions. And what made this moment even more dangerous was the sun was still low enough to create a blinding glare on windshields. Because of these combined factors, the tiny, pale girl with almost white blonde hair would likely never be seen by the motorists until it was much too late to stop.

As Yvonne drew closer to the highway, she began to run. She covered ten feet and then twenty about as fast as a toddler could. With no one close enough to now stop her trek, it was obvious the open gate had set in motion a series of events that would end with an accident too tragic to comprehend.

Though she was now stepping out into the street, the drivers of a car and truck coming toward the intersection never saw the little girl. With huge chrome bumpers and thousands of pounds of steel just a few feet away, Yvonne was about to make a second step, this one likely fatal, when Lulubelle reached forward, grabbed the toddler's dress, and yanked the child back onto the sidewalk. The dog then knocked the girl to the ground and sat on her. No matter how loud the screaming child yelled or how hard she kicked, the fifty pounds of fur would not budge.

The woman who had witnessed the amazing event play out from the porch spun her wheelchair around and pushed it into her home. Cranking her phone, she rang the operator who called the Herns' house. Two minutes later a frantic Wilma arrived at the scene to find Yvonne still pinned to the ground by a dog that somehow realized the tactic was the only way to keep the little girl safe.

After a great many tears and hugs, Yvonne spent the rest of the day in trouble. Wilma drove home the point again and again that the little girl could never, under any circumstances, leave the yard alone. Meanwhile, Lulubelle was treated like a queen. From the refrigerator and cupboard came treats the dog thought were only reserved for humans. That night, when Hugh got home and heard the story, the mutt received even more praise and food.

The next day, and every day thereafter, Hugh made sure the gate was shut and locked before he rode off to work, but as far as the dog was concerned the man's diligence was for naught. That street corner where she had saved a child's life called out to her and when the gate would not open, she taught herself to climb the fence. As the weeks went by, the dog continued to escape from the yard early in the morning and again in midafternoon. It was as if she was on a mission. And, as it turned out, she was.

Each morning and afternoon, Lulubelle beat the neighborhood schoolchildren to the corner. She waited there until the guard stopped traffic to help the kids cross the street. If any of them left early, she yanked them back. When the guard signaled for the kids to move and they walked into that dangerous intersection, she marched out with them, defiantly sitting in the middle of the road, staring down traffic in all four directions until every child had made it to the other side. Then and only then did she move back to the corner to wait on the next band of students. She would continue her mission in rain, sleet, sunshine, and snow until Hugh was transferred to another city and the family moved.

Simply by saving a child's life, a collie-shepherd mix discovered a calling. She locked onto that need and would not let go. Nothing could keep her in the yard and away from her work. How many lives did she save? Only one can be documented, but it might have been many more because there were days when she was there and the crossing guard was not, and even then she marched out and stopped traffic so the students could safely cross.

Oprah Winfrey once said, "I believe there's a calling for all of us. I know that every human being has value and purpose. The real work of our lives is to become aware. And awakened. To answer the call." As the stories in this book prove, not only people look for callings, so do dogs. And each day, by simply answering their callings, our dogs save lives, teach great lessons, bring dynamic inspiration and, ironically enough, help guide each of us to become better human beings. The most important moral found in the lessons presented in this book is the world we live in just might be a much better place if we were all a bit more like man's best hero and a little less like man.